Crypto Uncovered

Sarah Swammy • Richard Thompson
Marvin Loh

Crypto Uncovered

The Evolution of Bitcoin and the Crypto Currency Marketplace

palgrave
macmillan

Sarah Swammy
State Street Global Market, LLC
New York, NY, USA

Richard Thompson
Digital Air Technologies
New York, NY, USA

Marvin Loh
Bank of New York Mellon
New York, NY, USA

ISBN 978-3-030-00134-6 ISBN 978-3-030-00135-3 (eBook)
https://doi.org/10.1007/978-3-030-00135-3

Library of Congress Control Number: 2018961381

Cover illustrations: Westend61 / Getty Images
Cover design by Tjaša Krivec

This Palgrave Macmillan imprint is published by the registered company Springer Nature Switzerland AG
The registered company address is: Gewerbestrasse 11, 6330 Cham, Switzerland

Foreword

Sovereign fiat currency may one day be considered pocket change and what is today's crypto currency may become the basis for tomorrow's sovereign digital currency. Regardless of how soon this happens, one thing is certain: blockchain is the technology that will provide the ubiquitous digital portal through which all financial transactions will occur. While the markets in crypto currencies have been roiled by huge swings in recent valuations and while there are clear and present dangers for investors in these currencies, this underlying technology and the driving forces for the emergence of stable digital currencies *are* here.

Many people think of crypto currency versus canonical fiat currency. But, this comparison misses a crucial point about the latter, which is that most of our money and our transactions are fully electronic already. When was the last time you went to the bank to check on your money in their vault? So, it will not be as huge a jump as some may think for consumers and governments to move from where they are today with electronic finance to purely digital currencies. Having a digital currency become a nation's sovereign currency and disintermediated by way of blockchain technology is very intriguing. Do we really need a bank between us and our money in the not too distant future? Crypto currencies may have a long road to travel if they are to ever *replace* the dollar or the euro but the transition to nationally denominated, sovereign digital currencies that are open, honest, and unconcealed, but secured by blockchain may happen sooner than many suggest or expect.

We are already seeing enormous investment in this new digital currency among the biggest and oldest financial institutions in the US. In July 2018, *Forbes* reported that Northern Trust has begun to integrate crypto currencies into several areas of business to create and more efficiently manage tradable digital assets.

"You can take anything today. You can take movie rights, you can take all sorts of entities, and you can create a token for those," Pete Cherecwich, president of Northern Trust's corporate and institutional services, told *Forbes*. "We have to be able to figure out how to hold those tokens, value those tokens, do those things."

Although Jamie Dimon, CEO of JP Morgan Chase, has professed no interest in crypto currencies, they are now attracting greater attention from many other traditional financial institutions and investors. In fact, KPMG reported in August 2018 that US investment in blockchain during the first six months exceeded all of 2017. The reason? Blockchain is no longer an experiment in crypto currency; it is the real deal with the potential to revolutionize the financial sector. But, just as assuredly, as digital currency gains momentum, we will see increased regulatory oversight from governments that seek to prevent market manipulation, reduce fraud, and minimize risk. China is a notable example of one nation that has recently and systematically cracked down on crypto currencies.

However, China is at the same time pushing forward with the underlying technology behind crypto currencies; the Chinese Ministry of Industry and Information Technology is looking to advance its adoption of blockchain to optimize its own financial industry and other sectors such as supply chain management. This is the "Jamie Dimon" approach and that of many financial institutions in the US and Europe, which is exemplified by a great interest in the underlying blockchain technology that fuels crypto currencies, while remaining skeptical about Bitcoin, Ethereum, Ripple, and other digital currencies themselves. Significantly, at the time of this writing, the Chinese Communist Party just announced that through its People's Daily Publishing House it has made available a book entitled *Blockchain—A Guide for Officials*, which is a primer on distributed ledger technology. This follows closely on the heels of an announcement by the Bank of China to invest more than 1% of its annual revenue in blockchain and other financial technologies.

Regardless of where the major players stand, one thing is clear: through crypto currencies, we are witnessing the promise of blockchain unfold in real time—the idea of massively distributed authentication and recordkeeping without the intermediary is incredibly disruptive in prospect. All of this may lead to financial ecosystems that are safer, more privatized, and more efficient.

The potential for blockchain to disrupt our world goes well beyond crypto currency, banking, and finance. It could come to the rescue of faulty science by authenticating and certifying published research data that surpasses peer review. In doing so, the scientific community could reduce errors (it is estimated that over two-thirds of experiments are unable to be replicated by other scientists).

As blockchain becomes more widely accepted as a first-rate credibility standard, researchers could post results online directly, thus enabling the scientific community to share information more quickly and more accurately.

The possibilities are unceasing: in higher education, blockchain can assess a person's competency by certifying skills, experience, and knowledge to future employers; in medicine, it can help reduce health care costs; and among government agencies, it may help reduce waste and overexpenditures.

The nascent yet intriguing realm of crypto currencies only ensures that blockchain technology will continue to attract investors, innovators, entrepreneurs, and educators. This last group will be essential in teaching the future generations of computer science and financial experts who will take us from today's "dial up" era of crypto currencies to a new era of stability, security, and sovereignty.

As the president of an academic institution focusing on technology writ large and more recently on blockchain technology in particular, I am proud that New York Institute of Technology (NYIT) alumna and co-author Sarah Swammy, as well as contributor and faculty member Steven J. Shapiro, have shared their expertise in this book to help readers better understand the past, present, and future potential of crypto currencies.

Blockchain technology will continue to evolve by building upon the technologies that led to its inception and innovation. Its evolution will accelerate at a faster pace. Perhaps, in contrast to how the internet and World Wide Web evolved, the unfolding of blockchain technology, crypto currencies, and their collective impact will follow a more managed and predictable evolutionary path course. Alternatively, they may evolve, adapt, and diversify spontaneously in new and very undirected ways. My Bitcoin is on the latter.

New York Institute of Technology
New York, NY, USA

Henry C. "Hank" Foley

Acknowledgments

We would like to express our enormous gratitude to our colleagues and friends. As leaders in the industry, your vision, experience, and technical knowledge helped to make this book successful: the Hon. E. David Burt, Dan Castro, Henry C. "Hank" Foley, Steven J. Shapiro, Denise Young Smith, New York State Assemblyman Clyde Vanel, and Dr. Chad Womack. Thank you for all of your contributions to this work. We want to extend a special thank you to Larry Harris and Colin Robinson. Larry and Colin, thanks for helping us with the editing.

Contents

1 **History of Money** 1
Sarah Swammy, Richard Thompson, and Marvin Loh

2 **Tales from the Crypt: The Dawn of Crypto Currency** 17
Sarah Swammy, Richard Thompson, and Marvin Loh

3 **Silk Road to Wall Street: Accepting Crypto Currency as a Tradable Asset** 29
Sarah Swammy, Richard Thompson, and Marvin Loh

4 **Crypto Currency: What Do We Know About Investment Performance and Risk?** 47
Steven J. Shapiro

5 **Managing the Crypto Marketplace** 61
Sarah Swammy, Richard Thompson, and Marvin Loh

6 **Crypto Currency: The Birth of an ICO** 85
Sarah Swammy, Richard Thompson, and Marvin Loh

7 **Creation of a Distributed Ledger** 133
Sarah Swammy, Richard Thompson, and Marvin Loh

8 ICO Regulatory and Reporting Framework 149
Sarah Swammy, Richard Thompson, and Marvin Loh

9 Crypto Currency: Another Block in the Continuum of Value Exchange 169
Dan Castro

10 A Vision for the Future: The Bermuda FinTech Story 173
E. David Burt, Sarah Swammy, Richard Thompson, and Marvin Loh

Notes on Contributors

E. David Burt, JP, MP is Bermuda's youngest premier. He is a graduate of the George Washington University in Washington, DC, where he graduated cum laude with a Bachelor of Business Administration with a double major in Finance and Information Systems. He was awarded the George Washington University Presidential Administrative Fellowship and received his Master's of Science degree in Information Systems Development in 2003. David attained a Project Management Professional certification in 2009. He is also a licensed private pilot. An entrepreneur, David started GMD Consulting Limited, an IT consulting company focusing on project management. He served as president from its inception until 2016 when he stepped down upon being appointed Leader of the Opposition. David co-founded HITCH Limited and was the lead developer for the award-winning HITCH Mobile App enabling Bermuda residents to hail taxis. In the past he has served on the Tourism Board, National Training Board, and as a director of the Bermuda Chamber of Commerce, and has been a director of the Bermuda Economic Development Corporation. David is also active in local and international public service and community organizations. He is a member of Alpha Phi Alpha Fraternity, Incorporated, the Western Stars Sports Club, and the Devonshire Recreation Club.

Dan Castro is the Founder of Robust Advisors, Inc., an independent consulting company focusing on structured finance markets, including Asset Backed Securities (ABS), Residential Mortgage Backed Securities (RMBS), Commercial Mortgage Backed Securities (CMBS), Collateralized Debt Obligations (CDOs), Asset Backed Commercial Paper (ABCP), Structured Investment Vehicles (SIVs), and other structured finance securities. Robust

Advisors provides due diligence, valuation, expert witness, litigation support, and general consulting services. Robust Advisors, Inc.'s clients include banks, broker-dealers, hedge funds, insurance companies, issuers, originators, rating agencies, and trustees.

Dan has been involved in the Fixed Income and Structure Finance Markets for over 30 years. His experience includes mortgage origination, underwriting, and servicing, mortgage banking, and broad knowledge of ABS, RMBS, CMBS, CDOs, Real Estate Investment Trusts (REITs), ABCP, SIVs, and other structured finance products. Dan has a particularly broad perspective on the market and has worked as a strategist, quantitative analyst, banker, rating agency analyst, research analyst, collateral manager, fund manager, Chief Investment Officer, Chief Credit Officer, Chief Risk Officer, salesman, and investor.

Dan has been on both the sell side and buy side of the market (buying and selling billions of dollars of ABS, RMBS, CMBS, and CDOs) and has a thorough understanding of both the big picture and nuances of the fixed income and structured finance markets. During the time Dan ran Merrill Lynch's Structured Finance Research Group (1991–2004), he was voted to the Institutional Investor All-America Fixed Income Research Team for 13 consecutive years, and was recognized for his expertise in ABS, RMBS, CDOs, and mortgage prepayments. He was the top-ranked analyst for ABS Strategy in the industry multiple times according to the Institutional Investor industry poll.

Prior to Founding Robust Advisors, Inc., Dan spent a year as Managing Director and Head of Strategy and Analytics for Structured Finance for BTIG LLC, a FINRA-registered broker-dealer. From 2008 to 2010, Dan was Managing Director, Chief Risk Officer, and portfolio manager at Huxley Capital Management. From 2007 to 2010, Dan served on the Board of Directors of the American Securitization Forum, an industry trade organization that represents the securitization industry. As an ASF Board Member, Dan provided expert advice and analysis to Congressional committees, the Federal Reserve, and the Department of the Treasury.

From 2005 to 2008, Dan was Managing Director, Chief Credit Officer, and a portfolio manager for the Structured Finance Group at GSC Group, an investment management firm that also served as a CDO Fund Manager. While at GSC, Dan was also the Chief Investment Officer of an REIT named GSC Capital Corp. From 1991 to 2004, Dan was Head of the Structured Finance Research Department at Merrill Lynch. Before joining Merrill Lynch, Dan was a senior analyst at Moody's Investor Service from 1987 to 1991, and chaired ABS and RMBS rating committees from 1990 to 1991. From 1984 to 1987, Dan worked at Citicorp where he was an analyst and banker.

Dan holds an MBA in Finance from Washington University, preceded by a Bachelor of Arts degree (B.A.) in Government from the University of Notre Dame.

Marvin Loh has 30 years of experience in the financial service industry where he has been an analyst at various firms covering a multitude of asset classes. At present, he follows global macro themes for BNY Mellon, where he evaluates asset valuations by looking for intersections within the foreign exchange, fixed income and equity markets, both domestically and globally. Prior roles have included the director of research at W.R. Hambrecht and Fidelity Capital Markets. Marvin has also been active in identifying disruptive technologies and business models, having contributed to various white papers over his career.

Steven J. Shapiro, Ph.D. is Professor of Finance in the School of Management at New York Institute of Technology (NYIT), where he is also the Director of the Center for Risk Management. His research interests include cryptocurrency pricing, risk, and returns; assessment of the risk of the shares of closely held companies; finance event studies; and applications of economics and finance to issues in litigation. Professionally, Steven has testified on damages in personal injury, wrongful death, employment, intellectual property, antitrust, and commercial litigation. He has experience conducting statistical tests of employment discrimination and competitive analysis in antitrust litigation. He is also experienced in valuing the shares of private companies, stock-based compensation (including employee stock options), and pensions. Steven holds a BA in Economics from the University of Virginia and an MA and Ph.D. in Economics from Georgetown University.

Sarah Swammy is a Senior Vice President and Chief Operating Officer for the Portfolio Solutions businesses in both State Street Global Market, LLC, a registered broker-dealer subsidiary of State Street Bank and Trust, and State Street Bank and Trust. Sarah joined State Street from BNY Mellon where she held several leadership positions and has held compliance positions at Deutsche Bank Securities, Inc., CSFB, and Barclays Capital, Inc. Sarah is the executive editor and contributing author *of The Capital Markets: Evolution of the Financial Ecosystem* and author of *Governance Compliance and Supervision of the Capital Markets*. She is an adjunct instructor at New York University School of Professional Services and serves as a member of New York Institute of Technology Advisory Board in the School of Management. Sarah holds a BS in Business Administration, an MS in Human Resources Management and Labor Relations from New York Institute of Technology, an MA in

Business Education from New York University, and a Ph.D. in Information Studies from C.W. Post, and is a graduate of the Harvard Business School Advanced Management Program.

Richard Thompson is the Chief Executive Officer at Digital AIR Technologies and Analytics, which he founded with the vision of marrying the immense power and scalability of modern cloud architecture with cutting-edge institutional business software to overcome technological challenges faced by enterprises today. With more than 20 years of experience directing the development of world-class institutional financial systems and pioneering the next generation of "cloud" technology, Richard is widely acknowledged as one of the foremost IT architects and technologists in the financial industry. Prior to Digital AIR Technology, Richard was Chief Information Officer and principal founder of Incapture Technologies, a director and front office systems designer/architect for Blackrock Solutions, and a director at Barclays Global Investors (BGI) for front office technologies. His many achievements include designing quantitative enterprise systems for Barclays Capital as head of the NY Derivatives Technologies and Trading Platforms, directing the development and implementation of BGI's fixed-income asset management system and creating front-office tools for BlackRock's Aladdin. Richard attended Cornell University for a program in Mathematics and Applied and Engineering Physics. He also attended NJIT for Master Programs in computer science and Carnegie Mellon University for a Master of Financial Engineering.

List of Figures

Fig. 2.1	Premier David Burt meets with executive team of Digital AIR Technologies & Analytics discussing blockchain and crypto currencies	27
Fig. 4.1	Bitcoin daily closing price, July 19, 2010, through June 29, 2018	51
Fig. 4.2	Bitcoin daily logarithmic returns, July 19, 2010, through June 29, 2018	51
Fig. 4.3	Bitcoin price, August 7, 2015–June 29, 2018	54
Fig. 4.4	Ethereum and Litecoin prices, August 7, 2015–June 29, 2018	54
Fig. 4.5	Ripple price, August 7, 2015–June 29, 2018	55
Fig. 4.6	Value of equal $1.00 investments in Bitcoin (BTC), Ethereum (ETH), Ripple (XRP), Litecoin (LTC), and cci30 Index, August 7, 2015–June 29, 2018	55
Fig. 5.1	Historical and forecasted number of Bitcoins in circulation	63
Fig. 5.2	Silk Road's three interconnected networks	72
Fig. 5.3	Metro Dog Training Center	74
Fig. 5.4	Roles in the dog care marketplace	75
Fig. 5.5	DOG token circulation data	77
Fig. 5.6	Actions in role	78
Fig. 5.7	Dog care business process	78
Fig. 5.8	Customer membership	79
Fig. 5.9	Service provider membership	79
Fig. 5.10	Compliance requirements	81
Fig. 5.11	Monitoring events and activities	82
Fig. 6.1	How crypto currency works	87
Fig. 6.2	Benefits of a smart contract	91
Fig. 6.3	Smart contract versus ESCROW	92
Fig. 6.4	LUCKY coin roadmap	96
Fig. 6.5	Sample token economics	100

Fig. 6.6	Traditional centralized application development	104
Fig. 6.7	Ethereum development model	105
Fig. 6.8	Truffle project	109
Fig. 6.9	Metamask wallet	120
Fig. 6.10	(a) Connecting to the Ethereum network. (b) Metamask accounts	120
Fig. 6.11	Browser display	121
Fig. 6.12	Adopt payment processing	122
Fig. 6.13	Lucky coin marketplace	123
Fig. 6.14	Minimum viable token	125
Fig. 6.15	ICO smart contract flow diagram	131
Fig. 7.1	Blockchain	134
Fig. 7.2	Block structure	136
Fig. 7.3	Mining process	137
Fig. 7.4	Mining rate management	138
Fig. 7.5	Mining process flow	139
Fig. 7.6	Centralized versus decentralized system	141
Fig. 7.7	Bitcoin price chart. (From CoinMarketCap.com)	142
Fig. 7.8	Crypto currency wallets	143
Fig. 7.9	Bitcoin transaction—real-world scenario	144
Fig. 8.1	Unique combinations of behavior	150
Fig. 8.2	Account summary	163

List of Charts

Chart 1.1	Payments type switch from cash to electric. (Federal Reserve Bank of San Francisco)	8
Chart 1.2	US trade balances (in billions). (US Census Bureau)	15
Chart 3.1	Interest in Bitcoin tracks and value of Bitcoin. (Source: Google, Bloomberg Finance L.P.)	30
Chart 3.2	Bitcoin and Ethereum: joined at the hip. (Source: Author using data from coinmarketcap.com)	32

List of Tables

Table 2.1	Contributions	18
Table 4.1	Crypto currencies with market capitalization of $1 billion or greater as of July 24, 2018, 10:59 AM, EST	49
Table 4.2	Summary statistics on daily logarithmic returns	52
Table 4.3	Correlations between daily logarithmic returns: Bitcoin, equity, bonds, and gold, July 19, 2010–June 29, 2018	53
Table 4.4	Summary statistics on daily logarithmic returns: Bitcoin (BTC), Ethereum (ETH), Ripple (XRP), and Litecoin (LTC), August 7, 2015–June 29, 2018	56
Table 4.5	Ratio of average daily return to risk based on daily logarithmic returns: Bitcoin (BTC), Ethereum (ETH), Ripple (XRP), and Litecoin (LTC), August 7, 2015–June 29, 2018	56
Table 4.6	Correlations between daily logarithmic returns: Bitcoin (BTC), Ethereum (ETH), Ripple (XRP), and Litecoin (LTC), August 7, 2015–June 29, 2018	56
Table 8.1	view_all_roles	161
Table 8.2	view_all_rolesByID	162
Table 8.3	view_all_users	162
Table 8.4	view_all_usersByID	162
Table 8.5	view_all_userByRole	162

1

History of Money

Sarah Swammy, Richard Thompson, and Marvin Loh

For the love of money is the root of all evil[1]
All money is a matter of belief[2]
Money makes the world go round[3]

As the above quotes indicate, money has been around for a long time, and some would argue since the beginning of time. Money is so common that everyone has experience with it and likely interacts with it on a daily basis. This familiarity does not, however, mean that money is universally understood. Therefore, we will begin by providing the following definition of money as described by the International Monetary Fund.

Money can be anything that serves as the following:

(1) Store of Value, which means people can save it and use it later
(2) Unit of Account, that is, it provides a common base for prices
(3) Medium of Exchange, something that enables people to buy and sell from one another

While crypto currencies do not necessarily meet all of the definitional requirements at the moment, they do represent a natural evolution of money. Additionally, many of the most appealing aspects of crypto currencies

[1] 1 Timothy 6:10, King James Version.
[2] Adam Smith (1776).
[3] From the musical Cabaret, 1966.

S. Swammy et al., *Crypto Uncovered*, https://doi.org/10.1007/978-3-030-00135-3_1

attempt to address many of the issues that have plagued money throughout history. From the perspective of these challenges, we will start by providing a brief history of money.

Barter

While one of the earliest forms of money is often considered barter, it actually falls short of the International Monetary Fund's definitional requirements for money. In a pre-currency society it is certainly easy to see how barter naturally evolves, with the baker looking to trade his bread for butchered meat as envisioned by Adam Smith in *The Wealth of Nations*. Of course, the limitations also become obvious as the baker has to first find a butcher interested in trading for bread before even determining the ratio of the two goods. These two parties also need to find farmers with wheat and ranchers with cattle that are interested in providing the baker and butcher with their inputs. While there are aspects of a medium of exchange, the requirements that bread (or meat) is a store of value and unit of account are not accomplished in this example.

These types of exchanges eventually gave way to a more standardized approach that facilitated a greater variety of transactions. Within each community, there were generally some agricultural products that were widely demanded by a large portion of that population, such as grain that could be ground or planted. In these instances, merchants of all kinds would be more willing to accept the broadly desired commodity if there was a general ability to exchange that product for something else. In our example above, while the butcher may not want bread, he would accept grain from the baker that could then be used to exchange for livestock from a farmer. The farmer in turn would be incented to accept grain as payment if it could be used to acquire tools from the blacksmith. These are broad examples of the development of commodity money, with salt, tea, and seeds widely accepted forms of "commodity money."

There are a few key points to take away from our example; firstly, grain has the potential to evolve into a unit of account and a medium of exchange, although its store of value is only as long as the grain does not spoil. An additional observation is that the success of grain as a currency is based on the broad-based belief in its convertibility into other goods and services. If that belief were suspended by enough of the community's population, the appeal of accepting grain would be hampered and only those that naturally needed it would continue to partake in this form of barter. This situation would then convert grain into just another bartered product that is limited by many of the issues described above. One last issue concerns the store of value, where a grain's shelf life is limited, but can also be broadly replenished on a year-to-year basis. In fact, a bumper crop may flood the market with grain that would lead to devaluation of that currency. As we shall see a little later in this discussion, this is akin to drastically increasing the supply of money, which in practical terms leads to inflation as there is a greater supply of currency available in the economy. For purposes of this chapter, we refer to currency as a medium of exchange, most closely associated with fiat currency issued by a central bank that generally has no intrinsic value. Money can be anything that fits the definition provided above.

Moving Beyond Barter

The Illustrious History of Shell Money

Functioning money in a format that we are more familiar with began to emerge at least several thousand years ago, with estimates in the 1000–2000 BC era. However, unlike paper currency or even metal-based coins, the earliest forms of global currency took the form of shells, more specifically cowry shells. It is understandable why someone may want to accumulate these shells as they are still aesthetically desirable as jewelry or for display. As a currency, these shells were appealing in that they were durable, relatively lightweight, and fairly unique looking, which guarded against counterfeiting.

Shells were therefore more appealing than cattle and grain in that they could be divided much more easily, didn't spoil, and were much more easily transportable. While cowry shells are most plentifully found around the warm waters of the Indian and Pacific Oceans, their role as currency is most closely tied with the Chinese adoption of the "currency." At the time, China had a vast empire and needed a way of facilitating transactions across a wide geographic region. In addition to the physical aspects of the shells discussed above, acquiring cowry in China was difficult given its distance from the harvesting fields. This gave Chinese emperors the ability to more easily control the supply of cowry in circulation and, by extension, the ability to control inflation.

While cowry shells are the most often cited form of shell money, they were by no means alone in their role within commerce. American Indians are often cited as using wampum, which is a string of small cylindrical beads made from quahog shells, as a medium of exchange. These examples also point to the durability of various clam and oyster shells that functioned much as cowry was used. Wampum was often strung together, which increased its appeal, although drilling, the process of cutting a hole in these hard shells, was a labor-intensive process for Indian tribes. In a way, this process naturally controlled the supply of marketable wampum in that while the shells were plentiful, converting them to tender limited the number of shells in circulation.

The arrival of Europeans and more importantly European tools permanently altered this relationship, however. The shells proved no match for metal tools, which allowed Europeans to produce tens of millions of wampum beads by the mid-seventeenth century. This effectively flooded the market with wampum beads, devaluing its worth and ultimately leading to the collapse of its usefulness as a currency. Nonetheless, shell money maintains a place in history as one of the longest lasting forms of currency, with examples of cowry shells being used as currency as recently as 1950s in various African markets.

From Shells to Coins and Paper

The next stage for the evolution of money was the introduction of coinage. Metal had been used as a medium of exchange almost as long as barter and shells, but the first minting of coins is thought to have occurred in the sixth or fifth century BC. The Lydians, an Iron Age empire that existed in parts of modern-day Turkey, are often cited as the first culture to introduce standardized metal coins. These early coins were likely created for ornamental purposes or as souvenirs, but were soon used as money. Further adoption and refinement saw standardized coins emerge in many cultures, including Greek, Persian, Indian, and Chinese societies.

Early coinage was made from electrum, a naturally occurring mixture of gold and silver. Other metals were subsequently utilized to make coins, including gold, silver, copper, and bronze. The use of these precious and semi-precious metals was by itself a store of value. Most cultures minted multiple sizes of all these metals, thereby allowing the facilitation of trade for all types of goods, big and small. The availability of precious metals also had an impact on the type of coins that were introduced. It was thought that some of the earliest pure gold coins were minted by the Persians as they held much of the world's gold at that time. In contrast, other cultures, such as the Greeks, did not have easy access to gold and chose to store their limited gold instead of converting it into coinage. Silver was therefore also widely used in coinage, particularly as gold became scarcer.

Gold and other precious metal coins ultimately gave way to paper money. That is not to say that gold has fallen out of favor, as we still have official gold coins being produced, such as the American eagle, Canadian Maple Leaf, and

South African Krugerrand. While coins fulfilled all of the definitions of money, they could still be cumbersome, particularly for large transactions. In addition to the logistics of carrying around large sums of metal coins, such practice also opened the bearer to theft.

Evidence suggests that paper money had its origins in China, as the invention of paper naturally gave way to the development of paper money. Dispersed and growing trade routes made transportation of large quantities of coinage increasingly challenging. Additionally, the limitations of coinage were evident either when there was not enough metal to produce currency needed to support growth or when inflation required the transportation of more coinage. The earliest forms of paper money were private transactions, where traders deposited their coins at their companies, which issued a promissory note based on this collateral. Governments eventually saw the benefits of issuing paper money, with broad introductions around the eighth century AD. Governments eventually established themselves as the only entity that could issue paper money, with the concept of the ministry of finance becoming formalized 500–600 years after paper money was first introduced.

The development of paper money was not without hiccups, however, as the temptation of unlimited printing of money eventually led to rampant inflation in China. Paper money was actually eliminated for several hundred years following an especially deep financial crisis. This entire life cycle of paper money in China occurred before the Europeans even considered issuing their own paper currency, even though Marco Polo reported on its use in the late thirteenth century.

Development in Europe followed a similar path, as banks held gold and silver for its customers providing a receipt promising the repayment of the collateral on demand. These notes then became demand notes for the bearer, making them an ideal vehicle in facilitating business transactions. The first official European note is credited with the Swedish, with the private Bank of Stockholm issuing notes backed by copper and silver holdings in collaboration with the Swedish government. Similar to the Chinese experience above, too many such notes were printed, which declined in value when the bank was not able to meet the demand of its depositors who wanted the return of their silver and copper. The bank eventually collapsed, was taken over by the government, while its founder was imprisoned within ten years of its founding. Sweden also banned the issuance of new banknotes until the eighteenth century.

Despite these setbacks, paper money continued to flourish although initially it was banks that were the primary issuers of paper money. The growth of international trade in the thirteenth and fourteenth century in Europe evolved with the issuance of notes that represented holdings of gold or silver at a depository. Initially these notes only entitled the depositor to the precious metals, but evolved to provide the bearer with the right to the collateral. Merchants then started to request multiple notes for their larger deposits as the concept of multiple denominations emerged.

Banks themselves started to issue banknotes that were backed by gold or other collateral that they held, which often resulted in floating more notes than were physically backed by collateral in their vaults. This was possible as banks did not expect all note holders to demand collateral at the same time, very similar to the modern banking system. Of course, as illustrated above, the temptation of issuing too many notes is ever present. In those instances, bank solvency becomes a problem for banknote holders, as was the case of the Bank of Stockholm. In the Swedish example, the Riksbank, or Swedish central bank, was established in the aftermath of this early crisis. Given that the monarchy was involved in the establishment of the Bank of Stockholm, which initially provided the venture with credibility, the Riksbank was established outside of the government, with the primary task of maintaining price stability. These principles became the foundation of modern central banks, and the Riksbank is considered the first and oldest central bank.

While Sweden is credited with the first banknote and the first running modern bank, out of caution, the Riksbank did not issue new bank notes for over 100 years after its establishment. During that time, other countries stepped in to fill this void and advance modern financial theories. England played a pivotal role in this sequence of events, but it was from a position of necessity that its financial innovations were first introduced. The English military was ravaged after a long war with France that required significant resources to rebuild. With credit tight, the Bank of England was established in 1694 to raise 1.2 million pounds in order to rebuild the navy.

Over the course of several hundred years, standardized banknotes issued by the Bank of England were first introduced. Counterfeiting also became rampant as private banks and the Bank of England both continued to print notes, causing some confusion as to which notes were real and which were fake. While the sentence for counterfeiters was death, fake notes continued to cause problems, leading to the Bank Charter Act that granted note printing monopoly powers to the Bank of England. The US printed its first government note in 1862 declaring it legal tender, meaning that they must be accepted to settle debts. These advancements in finance and the payment system have been largely replicated around the world.

As we will review the development and role of central banks a little later in this book, we will jump to some of the more important developments with regard to currency which paved the way for crypto currencies. Crypto has been a natural extension of the digitization of money, which began with the advent of the charge card. By way of background, a charge card is characterized mainly by the requirement that the balance be repaid in full by at the end of each month. Earlier versions of electronic charge cards were introduced by the likes of Diners Club, Carte Blanche, and American Express. Credit cards are distinct from charge cards in that they are essentially forms of revolving credit, with less than full payment due each month, with outstanding balances subject to interest charges. Earlier versions of credit cards were pioneered by large merchants, which evolved to general use credit cards in the 1960s.

While charge and credit cards began making consumers comfortable with the digital payment system, users were still accessing their money through traditional bank channels. They either needed to get cash to pay these bills or wrote a check in order to facilitate the payment. The ATM further advanced how we access money by tying our bank accounts to a card that contained our identifying information. The first ATMs started in Europe in the late 1960s but quickly spread around the developed world. The development of interbank networks further advanced easily accessing our money, while also making access to money outside our domestic markets possible. There are an estimated 3 million ATMs globally.

By combining the concept of credit/charge cards with the accessibility of our own money we evolved to the debit card. According to the Kansas City Fed the first debit card was introduced in 1972. Other historians assign the first debit card usage later in the 1970s as an alternative to using checks with merchants, which was a cumbersome process of communications between a bank and a merchant. Nonetheless, debit cards have been around for a while, although their use did not really begin to accelerate until the 1990s. While slow to start, debit card usage has taken off, particularly after the financial crisis, as credit became tighter and consumers more conscious of their financial position. At present, when measured by the number of transactions, debit cards are used more frequently than any other non-cash payment method, including checks and credit cards. Further evolution of the payments system all have an electronic component, and include the development of peer-to-peer payments systems such as PayPal, Venmo, and Square, although each of these examples ultimately ties back to a more traditional payment vehicle.

As e-payments grow, they are expected to ultimately exceed cash transactions. In many ways, this has already occurred, with cash payments used for only 1/3 of transactions, with checks and electronic methods accounting for the balance. Governments also appear to be taking sides, actively trying to reduce the amount of cash in circulation. For instance, the European Central Bank stopped printing €500 notes, although existing large denomination notes remain legal tender. In far more dramatic fashion, India demonetized its largest bills, the 500 and 1000 rupee note. Converted into US dollars (USD), these notes would be comparable to removing the legal tender associated with $10 and $20 bills in an essentially overnight announcement. This caused hardships for Indian citizens, especially the elderly and the poor, as currency became scarce and many of these groups did not have access to electronic forms money. This movement is also gaining steam, with certain factions encouraging the US and UK to eliminate the $100 and £50 bills.

The main argument for a cashless society is the role that cash plays in tax avoidance and other illegal activities. In the US, there is $1.4 trillion in paper money in circulation, mostly in high-value notes. This staggering amount equates to a typical family of four holding $13,000 in cash stuffed in cookie jars or hidden under mattresses. In contrast, other studies show that the average person holds only $60 in cash. Critics of cash would argue that the differences between these amounts are used to facilitate tax evasion or other illegal activities. There undoubtedly is some truth to these claims, although the appeal of cash also remains indisputable. As Chart 1.1 indicates, cash remains the main source of payments, with the largest, albeit shrinking market share according to analysis from the San Francisco Fed. When looking closer at the value of payments, cash's dominance is in the small-value arena, where it is used 60% of the time for transactions under $25.

While cash is money, as discussed above, money is much more than cash. What cash does provide are some unique and powerful characteristics within the payment system that other payment forms cannot replicate. Mainly, cash is universally accepted, is instantly cleared, and cannot be electronically hacked. It is, however, subject to government intervention, as was recently experienced by Indian citizens. As a national currency, money can also be

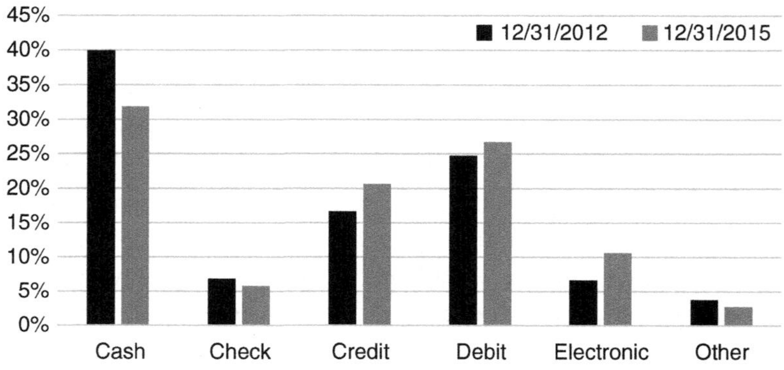

Chart 1.1 Payments type switch from cash to electric. (Federal Reserve Bank of San Francisco)

devalued by monetary and fiscal policies. Large transactions involving cash can also prove impractical, subjecting the parties to theft and/or increased scrutiny when large sums of cash make their way into the banking system. Lastly, cash is also anonymous, which provides solace in an increasingly connected and transparent global society. Crypto currencies have emerged as an alternative that potentially addresses the desire for anonymity in the payment system, while also providing many of the conveniences offered by electronic methods. As will be discussed in later chapters, crypto currencies have also been designed to protect from debasement created by government policies. Before we get there, however, we will look at a little more history and provide some of the more (in)famous failings of money.

The Role of Gold in Money

Gold has always played a pivotal role in the development of money from the start of currency transactions. It is one of the longest lasting forms of money if one considers that the earliest coins obtained most of their value based on the amount of gold they contained. National wealth was often measured by the amount of gold a country held, which had a direct relationship in European interest in exploring and often conquering the new world, often to gain access to its gold reserves. The discovery of gold in the Western US during the 1800s gave the US massive gold reserves, which provided the lever for US economic gains which contributed to much of the nation's modern successes.

The almost mythical position that gold has obtained occurred despite the metal's limited productive use. Initially, its use as a form of money was based on its non-corrosive nature, malleability, and aesthetics, which all made it a prime candidate as an early form for money. This could not be said of other metals, such as copper or iron, which corroded and therefore did not provide a store of value. Gold is also relatively rare, which gave it a leg up on silver in maintaining its value, but not so rare that it would impact economic development. It is worth mentioning again that money is only as valuable as the worth that society puts on any given currency. Therefore as long as gold maintained its value, it became increasingly valuable in the payment system.

Gold consequently played an important role in the development and acceptance of paper money. Earlier incarnations of paper money were simply deposit slips from institutions that held harder to transport versions of metal money. As governments became the predominant and then sole issuers of paper money, they initially maintained the tradition of having gold and/or silver reserves to back their currencies. It was not uncommon to have bimetallic currencies, although declining scarcity of silver ultimately created currency devaluation and market volatility for countries that maintained large silver reserves and relatively small gold holdings.

During the 1800s, most developed countries had moved toward using some sort of gold reserves to back their currency. England was once again at the forefront of currency innovation as it established the gold standard in 1821, formally tying its official currency to gold stocks. Slowly over the next 50 years, other countries followed suit, with France, Germany, and the US each backing their currency against gold reserves. This broad acceptance of the gold standard provided the platform for nations to cooperate on monetary policies. The period between 1871 and 1914 is often considered the height of influence for the gold standard, a time that was characterized by strong gains in global trade, limited inflation, and broad cooperation among central banks to maintain external balances at the cost of internal balances.

The basic concepts of the gold standard is one where an economy is adjusted based on price of goods, flow of specie, which was often gold coins or bars. As a simple example, assume that Country A is running a trade deficit with Country B. This would obligate Country A to transfer gold reserves to Country B in the amount of the imbalance. Shrinking gold reserves at A would cause its currency stock to decrease, while the amount of B's currency would increase. This would cause the price of goods at Country A to deflate, which would stimulate more exports, presumably to Country B. In turn, Country B would experience inflation as it has more currency in circulation. Given the weaker economy in Country A, and higher prices of Country B's goods, the trade imbalance would reverse. This ultimately creates a reversal of the gold outflows, changes the amount of currency in circulation, and brings the imbalance back into equilibrium.

Our example is a fairly simple example of the gold standard, but one that we can use to highlight key aspects of the system. Firstly, decisions around monetary policy are fairly limited, as the amount of gold ultimately dictates the amount of currency in circulation. Interest rates are important in that they should be used to help facilitate the ultimate movement of gold to bring external balances back to neutral. Imbalances can also lead to investment from gold-rich countries that improves productivity in weaker economies. While prices fluctuate, exchange rates do not unless the amount of gold in the global system changes. Since monetary actions are limited by gold holdings, governments are somewhat helpless when facing internal economic hardships. Inflation is generally held in check, but so is overall global growth, both limited by the finite stores of gold reserves.

It is no coincidence that this period of the gold standard ended in 1914, which coincided with the start of World War I (WWI). Trade imbalances had been growing for a while as serial deficit countries ultimately cheated on their obligations to encourage external rebalancing in an attempt to hold on to their gold reserves. A degree of distrust also limited greater amounts of investments from reserve-rich countries for trading partners that ran deficits. The economic hardships of WWI caused nations to suspend the gold standard, as many were forced to print money in order to finance war efforts.

Following WWI, many countries tried to reestablish their gold reserves, which were challenged by the much larger monetary base that the depleted gold reserves needed to back. There were several instances of hyperinflation across Europe, with Germany a notable case in that its economic disarray sowed the seeds for World War II (WWII). Other countries were forced to depreciate their currency relative to pre-war levels as the currency in circulation was not anchored by gold reserves. Most attempts to reestablish a gold standard failed, which led to a gold exchange standard. Under this plan, participating nations agreed to accept the USD and Great British pound (GDP) as a standard to settle international transactions as they became the first reserve currencies. This system required coordination between the Federal Reserve Bank and the Bank of England, which assured other participants of the expandability of the USD and GBP into gold. The system proved fragile as countries, nonetheless, attempted to hoard gold rather than hold the reserve currencies.

The Great Depression effectively ended the gold exchange standard, with some scholars blaming the system on exacerbating the depth of the depression. In the US the collapse of many banks during the depression created an environment ripe for gold hoarding. To address this problem, the US government passed several major laws that effectively made it illegal to hold gold. The first was the requirement that banks exchange all of their gold reserves into Federal Reserve notes. This was followed by the requirement that all residents exchange their gold holdings into Federal Reserve notes. These series of actions made it impossible to convert holdings into gold as it was illegal to hold any gold. The US government ultimately created the Fort Knox depository to hold its ballooning stock of physical gold.

Reviving a gold standard took yet another step backward with the outbreak of WWII. It wasn't until near the end of WWII that the allied powers started to consider how to rebuild the global financial system. In one of the most important agreements in modern finance, 44 nations agreed to again use gold as a standard for monetary policy, except this time it would be via the US dollar. The US emerged after WWII as the most powerful country in the world, without most of the reconstruction challenges that most countries faced. The US also held between 65% and 75% of the world's gold stores, providing the US dollar with a clear advantage over other currencies in international trade. Therefore, following a three-week meeting at Bretton Woods, New Hampshire, the Bretton Woods Monetary Management System was established. Under this system, countries would agree to maintain fixed exchange rates closely tied to the US dollar. If exchange rates moved outside a 1% band to the USD, central banks would intervene, either buying or selling their local currencies to reestablish the relationship. Both the International Monetary Fund and the World Bank were established as part of Bretton Woods to assist in maintaining the system.

In exchange, the US. would guarantee the convertibility of the USD into gold at a rate of $35 per ounce. Gold exchanges were established in the US and in London to allay convertibility concerns. The result was that the USD replaced the gold standard in settling international imbalances. This new system was seen as a way to remove some of the rigidity of a pure gold-based system, while also avoiding some of the exchange rate volatility that emerged during the intra-war period of the gold exchange system. The main goals of Bretton Wood were to foster stable exchange rates, eliminate competitive devaluations, and drive global growth. By all accounts the Bretton Wood agreement was short-lived, as it took over a decade to implement and cracks in the system began to form almost immediately.

The US, which had run trade surpluses against most of the world during the post-WWII reconstruction phase, started to run deficits in the 1950s. Dollar claims against gold reserves exceeded their actual supply by the 1960s. The Vietnam War, fiscal deficits, and rampant inflation in the US during the 1960s into the early 1970s essentially doomed Bretton Woods. While Presidents Kennedy and Johnson attempted to preserve the system, in 1971 President Nixon announced that the gold window was closed and that the US would no longer convert dollars into gold in what became known as the Nixon Shock. Other agreements between the world's largest economies attempted to reestablish a stable exchange rate following the Nixon Shock, but were generally unsuccessful as floating exchange rates emerged. While the USD was no longer the world's official exchange currency, its position as the world's reserve currency was already well established by 1971, a role it maintains to this day.

As currencies were no longer backed by gold after 1971, all currency became fiat money on that fateful day. The main attribute of fiat is that it is money that is deemed legal tender, but has no value other than that promise. Recall that gold or any other physical backing for money essentially limits the amount of money that can be produced. This is not the case with fiat, where a government can essentially print as much money as it sees fit. Printing too much money risks depreciating its value via inflation, where your purchasing power decreases. Printing excessive amounts of money may potentially result in hyperinflation, where the value of money can depreciate hourly in the most acute instances. Some of the most extreme examples of hyperinflation include the post-WWI German mark, post-WWI Hungarian pengo, and most recently the Zimbabwe dollar. In these examples, inflation often exceeded 10,000% per year, with examples of Germans using the mark for kindling wood given its inability to fulfill its role as a store of value. Despite these extreme examples, overall global inflation has fallen since the financial crisis despite large increases in the supply of fiat currencies by the world's largest economies.

Determining the Value of Money

The value of a country's money is now best defined via its exchange rate versus another country's currency. The US dollar remains the world's reserve currency and it is therefore the main pair member for almost all currencies, a position that emerged as part of Bretton Woods. For instance, it is common for two non-USD currencies to be first paired against the USD in order to facilitate a non-USD cross-currency transaction. In terms of how those values are determined, currencies currently freely float, are fixed to another currency, or use a hybrid of a free and fixed model, often called a managed or dirty float.

Most of the world's largest economies allow their currencies to freely float, with China's managed float being a notable exception. Under a freely floating currency regime, valuation is determined by currency supply and demand factors, which causes exchange rates to constantly fluctuate. A global foreign exchange market is estimated to trade $5.3 trillion in currencies daily and essentially functions 24 hours per day on practically every weekday. The benefit of having a deep and frequently trading market is that valuations reflect all current information and price change can generally avoid large market shocks in all but extreme circumstances.

The price of a currency in the foreign exchange (FX) markets is determined by the underlying demand created by international trade along with the speculative aspects created by traders looking to profit from price fluctuations. Export of goods and services creates the most obvious source of demand, as a supplier will generally wish to be paid in their local currency. In simplistic terms, the importer would need to acquire the foreign currency by selling their local currency in order to make payment for those goods and services. This creates demand for an exporter's currency, driving its value higher, while adding supply (selling) of the other currency, driving its value lower. However, bilateral trade may create demand on both sides and if there is an equal exchange of goods, the balance of trade is neutral and there will be no need for any change in FX rates from a trade perspective.

In the real word, balanced trade is a rare occurrence, with countries running trade deficits or surpluses, sometimes in sizable quantities for extended periods of time. Under a classic gold standard, changes in money supply would be dictated by the changes in gold reserves as a result of deficit and surplus balances. The changes in money supply in turn would expand or contract the respective economies, creating periods of greater wealth in one nation over another. The better performing economy would be able to consume more, while the citizens of the deficit nation would find their consumption curtailed. A good's prices and demand would ultimately be impacted, as the net importers return to balance through a combination of cheaper exports and less imports. Throughout this period, exchange rates would be unchanged as they are fixed to the value of gold.

Floating currencies provide a similar adjustment mechanism, although the exchange rate itself alters the supply and demand equation. In our simplistic example provided above, the country that is a net importer runs a trade deficit, while the export-driven country has a trade surplus. Focusing on the deficit country, the value of its money declines as there is less demand relative to the surplus country (as implied by their individual trade situation). The decline in currency value ultimately makes its goods cheaper to the outside world, which eventually brings the trade imbalance back into balance. The opposite is true for the surplus country as its stronger currency now makes its goods more expensive and therefore less desirable. It would see its exports subsequently fall, contributing to make the move neutral. Ultimately, rising or falling exports impact the wealth of a nation's citizens, which has clear political ramifications that makes our simple example purely theoretical and not particularly useful for determining the value of money in the real world.

Our above simple example can only work if goods and services are the only cross-border transactions that occur between nations. It also requires full substitution across goods; in other words, one country does not have a resource or competitive advantage over another nation. Lastly, it assumes that the surplus country would never want to hold excess currency of the debtor country. Of course all of these caveats do exist in the real world, which is behind the large trade imbalances that exist across numerous nations. As Chart 1.2 indicates, the US has run a trade deficit for over 40 years, with the imbalance between China growing to $400 billion annually. This imbalance has not caused the value of the USD to collapse and CNY to rise, as China has chosen to hold its excess supply of USD and reinvest it into US financial assets. As

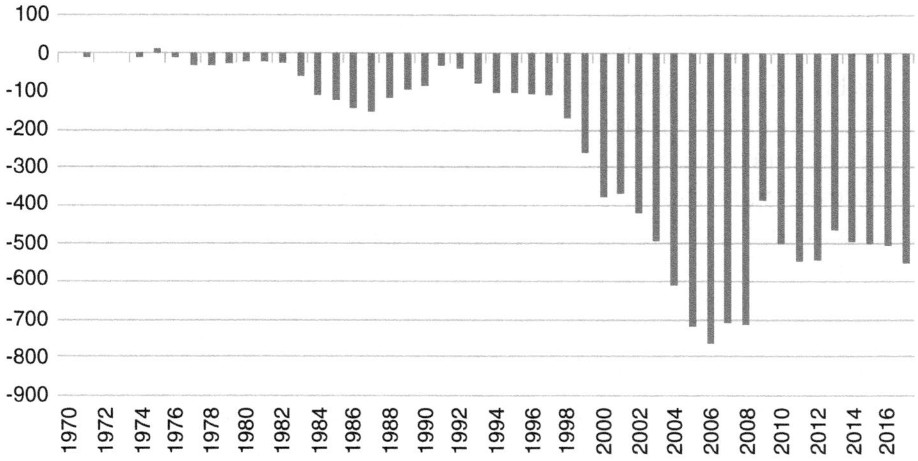

Chart 1.2 US trade balances (in billions). (US Census Bureau)

Chart 1.2 indicates, China's holdings of treasury securities presently exceeds $1 trillion, making it the largest holder of US government debt.

The world's willingness to hold US dollars is tied to its status as the predominant reserve currency, with the USD being used to price most of the world's commodities. The economic strength and rule of law of the US makes holding US assets appealing, which cannot be said for all countries. This serves to distort the simple trade-driven equilibrium mechanism that we presented above, and explains how a trade deficit can not only exist for an extended period of time but also accelerate during this period.

Monetary unions, such as the European Union, also highlight the challenge in using trade as the primary driver of exchange rates. Under a monetary or currency union regime, a set of countries agree to use the same currency. Since the single currency should reflect the collective performance of the union, individual country imbalances can last much longer than if individual currency regimes were maintained. In the case of the EU, the difference in the performance of the core and periphery countries is a prime example of these imbalances, which was responsible for the sovereign debt crisis that gripped the world in 2010.

As can be surmised, there are many factors in determining exchange rates, with inflation, terms of trade, interest rate differentials, outstanding debt, financial markets, government debt, and political stability just some of the obvious factors that we have not discussed extensively. Ultimately, while a currency reflects the strength of an economy and its citizens, there is a level when a currency gets too strong. In those instances, exports are curtailed, possibly increasing the odds of a recession, while also limiting inflation, which can impact wage growth. The response from a government may be to try and push its currency value lower, either by intervening directly in the FX markets or possibly through a lower interest rate regime.

Faced with a rising unemployment and/or a recession, central bankers have also attempted to stimulate their economies by increasing the money supply and lowering interest rates. These stimulative policies continue within some of the largest central banks despite our being ten years removed from the financial crisis. As interest rates were essentially set at zero in the world's largest economies, these same central banks started an unprecedented asset accumulation process, which grew the balance sheets of the G-4 central banks to over $14 trillion, a 250% increase from before the crisis. While the subsequent increase in their respective money supplies have yet to ignite inflation, there have been many periods of excess inflation being driven by large increases in the money supply. The inability to control these external forces has become one of the main appeals of crypto currencies, which by design avoids many of the monetary and fiscal pitfalls discussed above.

Bibliography

Federal Reserve Bank of San Francisco, https://www.frbsf.org. Accessed 16 June 2018.

Smith, Adams. 1776. "An Inquiry into the Nature and Causes of the Wealth of Nations," Cannan ed.

United States Census Bureau, https://www.census.gov/. Accessed 16 June 2018.

2

Tales from the Crypt: The Dawn of Crypto Currency

Sarah Swammy, Richard Thompson, and Marvin Loh

The price of Bitcoin hit an all-time high of $19,000.00 on December 17, 2017, sending the world into a frenzy about Bitcoin and crypto currency in general. Interest groups, media circles, and populations of people that appeared so far away from the discussion were now participating, driving the world into a state of frenzy concerning the crypto currency phenomenon. As many will discover, crypto currency is beyond a phenomenon. It is an innovative mode of conducting business that is here to stay. This staying power will be driven by reputable sovereign states, such as Bermuda, developing the legal framework for a working model to domicile initial coin offerings (ICOs) and by the prospect of the approximately 2 billion adults without traditional bank accounts discovering the virtues of crypto currency to perform everyday transactions through their mobile phone. Globally, approximately 1.1 billion unbanked have mobile phones that represents about two-thirds of the unbanked population.

Crypto currencies are digital money created by software programing using encryption technology. The digital coin is generated within a domain that connects a network of peer-to-peer computers.[1] These digital domains implement an immutable, distributed database called the blockchain which acts as the accounting system or official book of records for all transactions. The network utilizes a form of consensus model to verify transactions.

What makes this model unique is the decentralization of the accounting system. The model relies on cryptography (and unique digital signatures) for security based on public and private keys and complex mathematical

[1] Peer-to-peer network is a distributed architecture in which each node or computer has equal privilege as all the others in the network. And no coordination from a centralized computer is necessary.

S. Swammy et al., *Crypto Uncovered*, https://doi.org/10.1007/978-3-030-00135-3_2

algorithms. It runs on a decentralized peer-to-peer network of computers and "miners" that operate on open-source software and do "work" to validate and irrevocably log transactions on a permanent public distributed ledger visible to the entire network. This solves the lack of trust between participants who may be strangers to each other on a public ledger through the transaction validation work. The model enables the transfer of ownership without the need for a trusted, central intermediary, as exists in current financial systems. The incredible software engineers and mathematic, encryption, and engineering professionals who contributed to making such a platform should be applauded for laying the foundation for the innovation to come.

It should be noted that although Bitcoin is the first crypto currency to have achieved critical success, it was not the first crypto currency. The first digital cash platform to gain traction was DigiCash, founded by David Chaum, which relied on a system of "Blind Signatures" designed to ensure the privacy of users conducting online transactions. Chaum closed DigiCash in the late 1990s because he was unable to get enough merchants to accept DigiCash in order for consumers to use it.

There are more contributors in this space beyond the group associated with the David Chaum camp and the circle of cypherpunks. Recognizing some of the well-known pioneers brings insight to the conception and direction of where crypto currencies are derived from and where they can evolve in the future in their current form or as derivatives (Table 2.1).

Legal and policy developments in the 1980s around encryption also contributed to the birth of internet money. Prior to the 1980s, spy agencies were the primary users of cryptography. The internet being an open space with both private and public access resulted in the expansion and use of public key encryption technology. Two publications contributed to this expanded use of

Table 2.1 Contributions

Contributor	Contribution
Julian Assange	WikiLeaks founder
Bram Cohen	BitTorrent
Hal Finney	PGP 2.0 author, Reusable Proof of Work
Jacob Applebaum	Tor developer
Tim Hudson	SSleay co-author
Paul Kocher	SSL 3.0 co-author
Philip Zimmermann	PGP 1.0 creator
Bruce Schneier	Famous security author
Steven Schear	"Warrant Canary" creator
Dr. Adam Back	Hashcash creator, blockstream co-founder
Zooko Wilcox-O'Hearns	Zcash founder, DigiCash developer
Moxie Marlinspike	Open Whisper Systems

encryption tools: the US government "Data Encryption Standard" and "New Directions in Cryptography" by Dr. Whitefield Diffie and Dr. Martin Hellman, which set the process in motion to allow a framework for the government to allow access and use of cryptography for sectors outside the spy agencies.

Development of Bitcoin

These contributions and events laid the foundation for Bitcoin for Satoshi Nakamoto to revisit and inspired him to create a decentralized, immutable payment technology, free of double spending and providing privacy and anonymity to the users thereof. Users provide an encrypted address protected by public and private keys to maintain personal holdings, using the sophisticated network to transact and mint new coins through a software protocol.

Bitcoin Versus Fiat

With what can be implied as a ceremonious, symbolic, and successful launch of Bitcoin by one of its most prominent and mysterious pioneers, the infamous but never discovered, Satoshi Nakamoto, crypto currency achieved what would be the equivalent of landing a man on the moon in the cyberworld, as the statement revealed and imbedded into the Genesys block of the blockchain "The Times 03/Jab/2009 Chancellor on the brink of second bailout for Banks." The timing of the Bitcoin launch appears strategic and poses a direct jab at the modern-day banking systems as it comes on the heels of the near collapse and failure of large financial institutions such as Lehman Brothers and Bear Stearns. As pointed statements such as the Genesis block comment highlight, there is a competing relationship between centralized payment systems owned by the banks and decentralized payments owned by no one but managed by a peer-to-peer network of computers.

The natural comparison of crypto currencies to fiat currencies[2] always occurs. These comparisons do not have to be contentious in nature, with renowned banking executives denouncing crypto currencies a "fraud," only to later ignore earlier statements as they implement initiatives to include technologies powering crypto currencies for the strategic development of their own corporate strategy. That is why it is always important to separate the technology from those

[2] Fiat currency is money that a government has declared to be legal tender, but it is not backed by a physical commodity.

that run the technology. The technology that underlies fiat currencies is printing technology going back to early days of fiat currencies during the colonial period. It was the technology of the printing press to generate notes that were backed by the land of the issuing colony.

History of Fiat Money

A formal comparison of the evolution of fiat versus crypto currencies reveals that, from a compliance, governance, and control standpoint, crypto currencies' governance framework could mature much faster. Fiat currencies in the US started when the colonies began to print money to pay for debt owed as a result of the French and Indian wars. There was no oversight by the Royal parliament, and colonies created their own terms for delivering on the promise backed by these fiat currencies. The currencies also served as a means for a huge loss of revenue for the Royal government as colonists used it to pay Caribbean merchants directly, cutting out completely the tax revenue workflow implemented on goods by the parliament. Consequently, after a period of 30 years, Parliament issued the Currency Act of 1754, which nearly crippled the use of fiat currencies and almost made it impossible for colonists to do business and repay any debt, public or private.

Crypto currencies and digital currency technology are now becoming part of the global community and have a significant impact in developing countries. These include cases where the general welfare of communities and groups of people is improved, and they are a strong endorsement for the need of alternative financial mechanisms beyond the formal banking systems that primarily utilize fiat currencies as a medium of exchange. The financial digital frontier, initiated by the efforts of cypherpunks, is rapidly expanding and should be taken seriously by many sectors of society. For example, sovereign countries like Venezuela are exploring crypto currency backed by oil as an option to aid in providing a way out of the financial crisis.

When anyone compares the evolution of fiat currency and crypto currency there are strikingly similar phases that both monetary systems went through. When one carefully examines the origins of the system of fiat currencies it is easy to conclude colonists were printing money that had little real value to pay for the debt that was incurred by the British and American colonies to weaken the French power in Europe and expel the French from the American and Canadian colonies.

War was raging on both sides of the Atlantic in the late 1600s and into the mid-1700s with the official end recognized by the Royal proclamation of

1763. The French had conceded defeat and the Native Americans who were allies of the French during the French Indian wars were subdued. The treasury coffers of the British were severely depleted. Collecting debt from the colonies and exacting taxes were a means of revenue to replenish those coffers. As a means to overcome and deal with the mounting debt from war, the colonists printed money.

In those colonial times and early years leading to the formation of the US there were three primary mediums of exchange: commodity-based systems, species-based systems, and fiat systems. In commodity-based systems, colonists used the staples from the land as currency for business transactions. States that produced commodities that had a higher utility value, such as tobacco, had an advantage over states whose land did not yield such valued commodities. Virginia was one of those states that had such advantages, whereas states like Rhode Island did not. Species currency, a system that used gold and silver as the item of value, was greatly desired. However, species were scarce. Buying imports using species led to a flight of assets away from the commodity and depleted the supply. International factors limited the global supply and consequently led to a tightening of species as a means of exchange for business transactions.

The limitations of commodity-based and species-based monetary ultimately led to the increased practice of printing money and the development of the fiat system in the colonies.

This practice started with Massachusetts in 1690. By 1715, 10 out of the 13 colonies were actively printing money and using paper currency as a form of payment. It was so widely used that economist Stanley Finkelstein stated the advantages by saying "that unless it is backed by species it is cost free currency." The practice of indiscriminately printing money is problematic. It leads to hyperinflation and severe depreciation of the currency. That was the experience of the British merchants and creditors at the time who were paid for their goods and service with this depreciated currency, which they were not willing to accept. The mounting resentment of the British business community put increased pressure on the practice of the colonies printing these bills of credit to pay for debt, forced Parliament to declare the Currency Act of 1751, and led to a revision to the act in 1764.

During this nascent period of the fiat monetary system in the colony, Parliament, which was the central government during that time, permitted the colonies to implement an alternative monetary system outside of the British pound. This went on for about a 30-year period, where the colonial fiat system acted independently with no official oversight or rule. Apparently, the colonies did not seek input from parliament or any formal counsel to assist in advising to create rules of engagement for their alternative form of currency.

The colonists had created an alternative mode of conducting business using ink and the printing press, the technology of the time, to create paper notes of bills of credit. Now that they were able to conduct business and generate revenues, even though this was considered an illicit activity by the imperial government, the colonists were able to subvert the tax placed on sugar through the use of fiat money, thereby paving the way to create money by means of technology.

The printing press was the tool of liberation for the colonialist. Where the early settlers could use ink, the cypherpunks can use the internet as the technology of choice to produce an advanced form of money. The motive and spirit of the colonists and cypherpunks are similar, but the tools are different.

It is safe to say that Parliament or any central authority was excluded from the initial implementation of the fiat monetary system. This exclusion could have been a contributing factor to why the Currency Act was enacted severely against the colonial state governments. The colonies were prohibited from printing any money. The practice was discontinued and the colonies could no longer pay for private debt using fiat currency or bills of credit.

This declaration and issuance of the Currency Act resulted in a tightening of the money supply, which the colonists strongly opposed. Benjamin Franklin and other colonial agents went to London and opposed this act. Years had gone by without any acknowledgment from the imperial government. After years of lobbying by colonial agents, parliament issued amendments to the Currency Act of 1764 allowing certain states like New York to issue currency up to a designated limit.

There was another subtle by-product of the colonies' ability to print their own money: they could now pay vendors directly, subverting taxes imposed by the British. Goods like sugar could be bought directly from the Caribbean bypassing the British taxing agent. This flight of funds from the tax revenues was of serious consequence to the imperial power. All of these issues became factors that contributed to the revolutionary war. There were acts that were considered to be major grievances: three major ones were the Sugar Act of 1764, the Currency Act of 1764, and the Stamp Act of 1765. These acts guaranteed the enforcement of policy that violators would not be tried by a jury of your peers, but by the Royal parliament.

The First Continental Congress issued a Declaration of Rights that enumerated colonial objections to certain acts of parliament, and declared and labeled the Currency Act "subversive of American rights."

How Bitcoin and Crypto Currencies Can Change the Existing System

Technology directly challenges the government. It may for a time reduce some tax revenue streams as is evident by studying the evolution of fiat currency. However, government will catch up after carefully studying and instituting policies that will correct and bring in alignment all perceived lost revenues and will also protect the public from any threats that result from its use or practice.

This is not the case for banks. The technology is disruptive to the business model of the banking industry. Therein is the bone of contention between crypto currencies and the fiat centralized systems. Crypto currencies have a long way to go before they can compete at that level, where the market size ranges in the low hundreds of billions in daily transactions and fiat currencies is in the tens of trillions. However, it is something that cannot be ignored, as the public awakens and momentum gains. The modern-day banking systems left the door open for these currencies, which appeal to large groups of populations not able to participate within the purview of the traditional banking system.

Another subtle point not to be lost is the early period of flux in the evolution of the fiat system. The major benefit of the fiat system was provided to the Anglo-Saxon landowners. There were a little under 4 million people in the US by 1790. People enslaved represented a little more than 14% of the population standing at 690,000. The census count did not include Native Americans who accounted for about 600,000 people in continental US, dramatically down from the approximately 7 million estimated about the time of Columbus in 1492.

The fiat monetary systems in the early days of its existence excluded about 1.29 million people, who received little or no benefit from the system. It could be stated that the current fiat system started with a large underbanked or no-bank population. It is easy to understand theoretically why the virtues of the digital coin, inclusion principle, and democratization would resonate with a certain segment of society, in particular, the underbanked. It is obvious that certain segments of society were left out from directly participating in the fiat monetary systems, whether intentional or unintentional, and a large number of individuals received little or no benefit and that number significantly grew until the Civil War, when anticipated inclusion was a perceived promise.

In 1860 just before the beginning of the Civil War the US population grew to approximately 31,500,000, and the number of people enslaved represented 12% of the population with a census count of slightly more than 3.9 million, which is a significant number. The time right after the Civil War was a significant time of transition and promise. The hope of inclusion was symbolized by the creation of the Freedman Bank by Abraham Lincoln. A bank created to alleviate the struggles faced by formerly enslaved people, it helped to create a pathway of inclusion into the monetary system and capital markets of the time. However, that symbol of hope became a source of tragedy as congress voted to shut it down seven years after the assassination of Lincoln.

One can observe that the fiat monetary system has the ability to isolate and exclude segments of society because of the role given to banks to administer the execution of financial services to the consumer base. The pre-Civil War times and post-Civil War times are critical for the fact that there was no national system of banking implemented until the National Banking acts of 1863 and 1864 were issued by congress.

Banks were regulated by the states and there was no standardized system. The Polk administration started the movement toward a national system as public funds were taken out of private banks in 1846 and deposited into treasury branches. The establishment of a national banking system was just getting off the ground at the same time the slaves were being freed. There was no better time to establish a policy of inclusion and have a national monetary system that provided a venue for banks to grow and cater to all facets of society than immediately after the Civil War. The opportunity was extremely evident and there was no better time to unite the whole country. The failure of Freedman Bank and the consequent loss of hard-earned savings among the formerly enslaved caused deep distrust.

Crypto currency allows these issues to be brought to the table to heal and get rid of the glaring elephant in the room when referring to the unbanked and those excluded from access to capital and denied basic financial services because of policies of exclusion that have become endemic within corporate banking institutions.

Crypto currencies have not been free from their own share of controversies, especially surrounding the issue of Silk Road. The Silk Road case highlighted the fears of those critical of crypto currencies, being the means for criminals and illicit activity to run completely wild. The crypto currency world would insulate the so-called Den of Thieves with the promise of total anonymity and privacy free from any central authority. The Silk Road became an egregious marketplace where some criminal vendors had the audacity to display bricks of cocaine openly on the website.

Innovation can never be an excuse for allowing rampant criminal activity to be openly displayed in the face of any prosecuting agency. No society can survive with the exorbitant level of corruption that the Silk Road marketplace at that time offered with no oversight over any activity at all.

Ross Ulbricht indeed created a mechanism to facilitate illicit activities, such as narcotics deals, murder for hire, money laundering, wire fraud, and many other violations that could be charged in a federal court. Ulbricht was handed down five sentences served concurrently. Two were life sentences without the possibility of parole. Ulbricht did not personally commit the alleged crimes; however, his providing an enabling technology that leveraged Bitcoin as a medium of exchange allowed the prosecutor and the legal system to make him a poster child for the judicial system and for government officials to send a strong message that any violation involving crypto currency would be dealt with severely.

Severe prison sentences are usually enough to dissolve movements. This black cloud that was cast over crypto currencies was a correction and a catalyst for further innovation, adding revolutionary features of smart contracts to the already revolutionary and disruptive technology of blockchain.

The ominous cloud of criminality was blown away by the collaboration of technologists, finance professionals, and legal professionals that created the framework of laws to prosecute violators that used crypto currency, moving into advisory positions to assist entrepreneurs that are involved with crypto currencies as their core business. The crypto movement picked up a strong crosswind with the collaboration, advancing the movement and intensifying the acceptance of crypto currency in cultural and retail communities. Crypto currencies have evolved in the investment arena with some hedge funds taking strategies with the volatility of the price of Bitcoin and many of the popular crypto currencies.

The journey of understanding crypto currencies also involves the reason why currency fiat or crypto is used in general. People do not want to carry large quantities of species like gold or silver around every time they want to do a simple transaction at the merchants as it would increase the chance of robbery. Fiat and crypto currencies solve this issue. However, fiat is still physical in some situations, especially for the unbanked. In many instances they face being robbed and in harm's way when criminals know the cycle of when physical checks are cashed at non-bank entities they are forced to use.

The unbanked appears to be a growing population that will continue to benefit and build economies that do not exist today under a modern banking society as crypto currencies offer the alternative. Examining reasons for using currency and focusing on three primarily:

- Medium of exchange
- Store value
- Use money to make money

are areas that crypto currency will continue to evolve. Digital currencies will continue to grow in user experience from the marketplace offered by the Silk Road to mobile user experiences that will offer payment services from mobile phones. End users in remote areas will benefit using their phone and crypto currencies as the form of payment for daily transactions.

With respect to the store of value, volatility is a major issue of concern with crypto currencies. One factor that will take shape as ICOs are onboarded through foundations is that the use of the data from the blockchain which powers the technology will become of great value. The utility of the tokens along with the commercialization of the data which will contain transaction data makes it possible for a model to be created in conjunction with the foundation, thus begin to reduce volatility with certain digital currencies.

Using digital currencies to make money involves trading and having a professional background and qualifications to do so. This is where things become dangerous as some individuals get caught in the hype surrounding price growth of crypto currencies over the last four years, such as the increase in the price of Bitcoin, Ethereum, Litecoin, Ripple, and many more. There are more than 300 different currencies available. However, trading crypto currencies or any other asset or security, although crypto currency is technically not a security, requires professional training. It is easily to be enticed with the practices of "fear of missing out" and "pump and dump" that happen in the equity trading space and FX space in crypto currency.

To protect the public, government regulators are actively building legal and working frameworks to manage these innovating digital technologies. The first set of policies involves putting procedures around money service businesses (MSBs) to curb money laundering or fraudulent activity to protect public interests. Government agencies will conduct workshops and employ consultants to build internal knowledge banks around the subject matter, which involves hiring specialized consultants and training to help design effective working frameworks that will not hinder innovation of the technology, but bring a compliance structure to protect against anti-money laundering (AML), and limit criminal activity and suspicious activity such as payments to terrorist organizations.

Governments along with the banking industry are upgrading their talent pool and hiring resources that are experienced with the underlying technologies that power crypto currencies.

The Island of Bermuda is an example of a sovereign government that has been proactive in creating laws and a working framework for defining crypto currencies and conducting a crypto currency business; the country has instituted a reasonable and strict compliance program to deter any AML and

Fig. 2.1 Premier David Burt meets with executive team of Digital AIR Technologies & Analytics discussing blockchain and crypto currencies

fraudulent transaction activity. As shown in Fig. 2.1 Premier David Burt met with the executive team of Digital AIR Technologies & Analytics to discuss blockchain, crypto currencies, and artificial intelligence. Bermuda has created a legal framework that streamlines the ICO process as it looks to create the "Gold Standard" in domiciling ICOs.

Governments will have an instrumental role in managing the engagement between centralized and decentralized payment networks. Displacing the banking system is not realistic in any sense. Central banks have a role to play with the economic health of any society. However, technology and software has created an option for certain segments of society to supplement or in certain cases to become their primary choice for a medium of exchange when central banking is not feasible or at their disposal. As governments gain more knowledge and discover how digital currencies are positioned to complement the formal monetary system of the sovereign state, they will institute compliance frameworks that do not impede innovation. However, consumer protection against corruption, AML, and fraudulent activity will not be compromised.

3

Silk Road to Wall Street: Accepting Crypto Currency as a Tradable Asset

Sarah Swammy, Richard Thompson, and Marvin Loh

Trading in crypto currencies firmly entered the mainstream in 2017 posting some of the most staggering returns ever seen in the financial markets. By all accounts, the 1300% return for Bitcoin in 2017 would put it within the annals of one of the best returning asset classes ever, were it not for the much larger gains posted by smaller and newer virtual currencies.

As the value of crypto currencies has ballooned, so has interest in them. As Chart 3.1 indicates, google searches for the term "Bitcoin" have followed as meteoric a rise in interest as the value of the currency itself. It is therefore no surprise that the number of blockchain wallets doubled in 2017, exceeding 20 million by the end of the year. Holders of crypto currencies also found it easier to spend their coins, with the number of businesses accepting virtual money growing 40% during the year to over 11,000.

This certainly has led to more commercial transactions, with a counter maintained by blockchain.info indicating between 150,000 and 200,000 daily transactions during the second quarter of 2018. While these figures undoubtedly would also show impressive growth, they still pale in comparison to the 150 million transactions that Visa alone processes each day. Ironically, the recent success of and interest in crypto currencies is impacting its ability to fulfill key tenets of a successful currency. More specifically, the volatility in the value of crypto impacts its store of value, which in turn limits its use as a medium of exchange. The easiest way to think about it is if a merchant sells an item for a set level of Bitcoin, and the value of Bitcoin falls significantly, the merchant has effectively lost money.

This is no wonder when one looks at the returns posted by some of the largest cryptocurrencies in 2017. As mentioned above, the value of Bitcoin

S. Swammy et al., *Crypto Uncovered*, https://doi.org/10.1007/978-3-030-00135-3_3

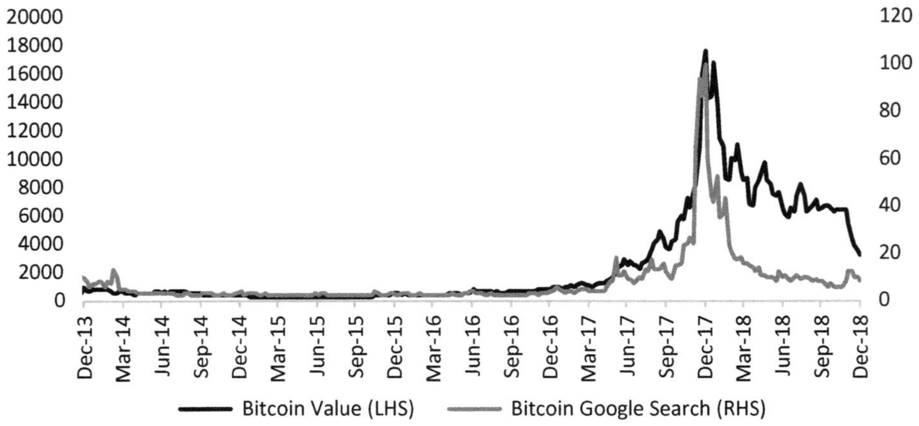

Chart 3.1 Interest in Bitcoin tracks and value of Bitcoin. (Source: Google, Bloomberg Finance L.P.)

increased by 13× in 2017. While spectacular, this almost appears paltry compared to the 8900% increase in Ethereum and 36,000% increase in Ripple. With rises and falls that have been spectacular on a day-to-day basis, it is no wonder that merchant acceptance has not been more robust.

This makes a large portion of the recent crypto convertees interested in the speculative nature of the asset class rather than in promulgating its usage as an alternative currency. The process of purchasing crypto has become far easier in the past several years, with well over 200 exchanges that facilitate the purchase and sale of crypto coins. Its popularity has resulted in several exchange traded funds (ETFs), which allows investors to obtain exposure to specific currencies as well as indices that track a basket of crypto currencies. Other ETFs track the underlying companies that provide blockchain services, while various futures contracts are available on the well-established Chicago Board of Exchange (CBOE) and the Chicago Mercantile Exchange (CME). There is no lack of ways to invest in practically all aspects of crypto currencies and their associated technologies these days.

Trying to Determine Value

With trading of crypto currencies evolving into one of the main reasons that investors own them, determining valuation is a key aspect of the investment process. The development of broad and liquid financial markets will go a long way in helping set a value for the numerous crypto currencies that are actively traded. One of the major roles for the financial markets is the price discovery process, with the interaction of buyers and sellers establishing a clearing price for financial assets. As more buyers and sellers meet in the marketplace, the market becomes more robust, or "liquid" in market jargon. A more liquid market would result in better price discovery, narrowing spreads, and ultimately greater trading volumes. New information would be quickly incorporated into prices, and relatively stable market-neutral prices (to a degree) would ensue until new information on the security entered the marketplace.

What we have witnessed in crypto currency trading is far from the above descriptions of an efficient market despite the large influx of new participants. The volatility of prices, both higher and lower, indicates the challenge of establishing a base value for the asset class. The recent fall in Bitcoin brings the losses in the currency to 80% since the start of the year, highlighting the speculative nature of the currency. This is somewhat due to the unique nature that crypto currencies occupy in the investing world as much of its evolution as a currency remains in the future. In the interim, its position as a virtual currency and/or evolving technology makes applying traditional valuation metrics difficult.

For instance, Bitcoin's initial development was to create a virtual currency without borders. Currency strategists generally rely on metrics such as currency account positioning, inflation, interest rate differentials, and a country's overall global standing in setting an exchange rate. Since none of those metrics are applicable and there is still limited actual commerce being transacted with Bitcoin, its value appears to be mostly determined by the speculative forces of supply and demand.

Somewhat in contrast to the goal of Bitcoin is the broader commercial applications of Ethereum and its smart contract brethren. To be sure, exploiting blockchain technology has generated as much if not more interest than Bitcoin's virtual currency aspirations recently. With both established and emerging stakeholders embracing smart contracts and the flexibility offered by blockchain 2.0 technology, the process of determining valuation for these firms should be different than trying to set a price on a virtual currency. However, as Chart 3.2 indicates, both Bitcoin and Ethereum values have moved in similar fashion over the past year, indicative of the influence they have on each other. For the moment, most of the larger crypto currencies are moving in unison both upward and downward as the general perception over the asset class is the primary driver for prices.

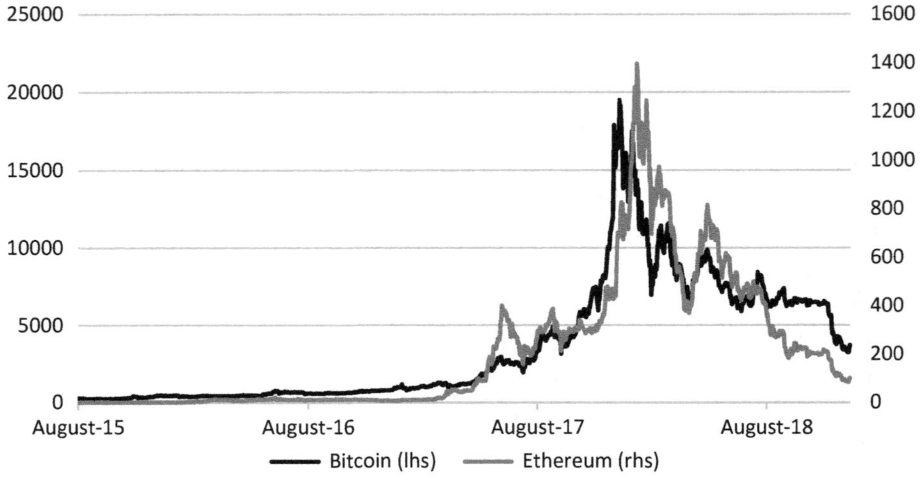

Chart 3.2 Bitcoin and Ethereum: joined at the hip. (Source: Author using data from coinmarketcap.com)

Important Developments in the Evolution of Trading Crypto Currencies

There has been no lack of key dates and events in the relatively short history of crypto currencies. It is easy to forget that until recently there was only one crypto currency (Bitcoin) and the first transaction is thought to have occurred in 2010 (10,000 Bitcoin for a $25 pizza order). From those humble beginnings, we have seen Bitcoin rise to almost $20,000 per coin and subsequently fall back to $4000, while there are now over 1500 crypto currencies to select from. The meteoric rise in all things crypto in 2017 pushed the market capitalization to over $800 billion in late 2017 from less than $20 billion at the start of the year. While the market cap has fallen to just over $100 billion recently, further technological advancements and investor interest will keep the crypto markets volatile, creating opportunities for those able to deal with the price swings. We have compiled a list of the most significant headlines and developments for the crypto asset class and its impact on valuation:

June 2011:	Gawker draws attention to Bitcoin's role in the silk road, ironically providing some credibility to the role of crypto currency as a medium of exchange, even if it was for illicit activities. Value rises 80%+ following the article.

June 2011: Mt. Gox is hacked for the first time, impacting an estimated $8.5 million worth of coins while temporarily crashing the price of BTC to $0.01. Mt. Gox was subsequently off line for over a week and the value of BTC collapsed by 80% during the summer of 2011.

March 2013: A software update proved incompatible with large sections of the BTC network causing the community to implement a hard fork back to the prior version that was supposed to be upgraded. Several large mining firms agree to forgo some mined coins to facilitate the version downgrade and there was little immediate impact on prices, although the value of BTC increases by 40% in the weeks following the event.

March 2013: Cyprus financial crisis is orchestrated between the country, ECB and European Union. The imminent collapse of the Cypriot banking system requires a bailout that taxes larger valued bank accounts and international accounts held in the country. The ability of Bitcoin to operate virtually outside of the rules established by governments and their central banks is immediately recognized by the financial community as its value doubles in the week following the bailout.

October 2013: Silk Road is effectively shut down, with the arrest of Ross Ulbricht, its owner and operator on money laundering, computer hacking and narcotics trafficking charges. As part of the arrest the FBI seized 144,000 Bitcoins, which was subsequently sold in various blocks in 2014 and 2015, netting $48 million. Following the arrest of Ulbricht in late 2013, the value of Bitcoin shuddered momentarily before surging over 5× in the following month. As an aside, 144,000 Bitcoins was worth almost $2.7 billion at the end of 2017, which while massive, pales in comparison to the $1 trillion U.S. government deficit that is forecasted for 2018.

November 2013:	U.S. Senate and Peoples Bank of China provide cryptocurrencies with some legitimacy by not declaring them an enemy of the state. U.S. Senate hearings acknowledge the innovative nature of the technology, while the then deputy governor (now Governor) of the PBOC stated that people are free to participate in the Bitcoin market. China has become a hotbed of Bitcoin interest in light of the tightly controlled exchange limitations placed on the Country's currency, the Renminbi. The value of Bitcoin rises from $208 to $1,140 over the course of the month.
December 2013:	As quickly as China provided the market hope, it backpedals as the PBOC declares that Bitcoin is not a currency and forbids financial institutions from doing any business with the cryptocurrency. After topping out at $1,130, the value of Bitcoin falls to $500 in the week following the announcement and does not recover that valuation again for over 3 years.
February 2014:	Early 2014 proved to be a challenging year for Bitcoin exchanges with several struggling from hacks and/or external attacks. Mt. Gox proved to be the most vulnerable, as it was hacked for nearly 1 million coins, forcing it to file for bankruptcy by the end of February. The value of Bitcoin fell by almost 50% to a low of $450 near the end of the month.
August 2016:	Bitfinex, the largest cryptocurrency exchange by volume, is hacked for 120,000 Bitcoin. The price of Bitcoin is fairly stable following the news, although its value had fallen by 15% in the days prior to the announcement, raising the specter of insider information.
April 2017:	Japan becomes the first country to recognize Bitcoin as a legal payment method. Possibly in response to the collapse of Tokyo based Mt. Gox a few years prior, or an attempt to play a bigger role in the emerging fintech space, Japan has moved to the forefront in the cryptocurrency

debate. It is worth noting that while Bitcoin is recognized as a legal payment method it is not considered legal tender. There are also many unanswered questions for holders of cryptocurrencies in Japan, where they are treated more like an asset than a commodity. Nonetheless, Bitcoin has become resurgent in 2017, rising 30% in April to an all-time high of $2,400 that month.

September 2017: China sours on the unregulated aspects of cryptocurrencies, first banning all ICOs in the country in early September and then shutting down all cryptocurrency exchanges later that month. This led to concerns amongst the country's mining community that they would be targeted next, which ultimately occurred at the start of 2018. In terms of market reaction, Bitcoin initially fell 30% during the 1st ½ of the month, before recovering 70% of that decline by month end.

October/December 2017: Chicago Mercantile Exchange and the Chicago Board of Options Exchange announce and eventually offer the first Bitcoin futures contracts, with the approval of the U.S. Commodity Futures Trading Commission. There is a surge of new entrants into the market, with Coinbase reporting 100,000 new users after the CME announcement. Prices surge in November and December, with Ethereum rising 5× and Bitcoin up 3× in the final 2 months of the year.

May/June 2018: Market manipulation comes into focus, with the U.S. Justice Department opening a criminal probe into whether traders used tactics such as spoofing or flooding to influence prices. A University of Texas paper authored by Professor John Griffin and Amin Shams also credibly argues that price manipulation was responsible for at least 1/2 of 2017s rise in cryptocurrency values. Valuations have been weaker all year, with Bitcoin down 30% in May and June and 70% since hitting a peak in mid-December, 2017.

June 2018: Coinrail, a crypto exchange based in Korea, was hacked for $40 million worth of alt-coins. Neither Bitcoins nor Ethereums were apparently stolen, but both cryptocurrencies fell over 10% on the news as it contributed to the negative tone in the market. This event is notable in that other crypto currencies were stolen as part to this hack, but the valuation of all cryptocurrencies were impacted.

As the historical review reveals, there has been no lack of positive and negative news impacting the development and trading of crypto currencies over the past several years. Some of the patterns that emerge are that any movement toward wider acceptance of crypto currencies either as a currency or as a technology has been embraced by investors. The growing pains have also been evident with hacks and market manipulation suppressing interest and prices through various periods of the crypto evolution life cycle. Most recently, the decline in prices in 2018 has reduced broader investor interest and will likely reduce broader commerce applications in the short term. Through this, it also appears that the crypto space has become more resilient, and while prices are down 80% from their all-time highs as at the time of this writing, they are still over 4× higher than where they started in 2017.

While many of the new entrants into the crypto market have been drawn to the possibility of quick profits, an extended period of calm is likely one of the best things that could happen for the space. Some of the most influential developments listed above came when it was realized that Bitcoin could be used as a medium of exchange, albeit initially in the illicit sphere of the Silk Road. Further validity was provided during the Cyprus banking crisis, as the borderless, dis-bursed nature of the crypto currencies directly addressed the risk of centralized controlled money. The price volatility we ultimately experienced since 2017 works against further advancements on this front, while bringing greater and somewhat warranted regulatory scrutiny. There will undoubtedly be many more twists and turns for crypto currencies, although investors should be cognizant of the risk that short-term volatility may have negative longer term implications.

Nuances in Trading Crypto Currencies

The growing popularity of crypto currencies has made it far easier to buy and trade your favorite virtual currency. Just as we have seen the number of crypto currencies expand from 1 a decade ago to over 1600 today, we have seen a similar evolution in the number of trading venues. In the early years, there was only Mt. Gox, whose failure highlights the risk to both the asset class in terms of damaging its reputation and the individual investors that lost their money. The growing interest in crypto currencies has resulted in the multifold increase in trading venues over the past few years, with between 200 and 500 crypto exchanges globally.

How Trading of Traditional Financial Securities Is Structured

In the traditional financial markets, investors generally need to open a brokerage account with a firm that provides the services and the interaction that the investor desires. If they want to simply trade stocks at the lowest price, there is no lack of discount brokers to pick among. A higher touch relationship may require a full-service firm that has a venerable name and reputation that makes one comfortable. Each one of these traditional businesses can, nonetheless, access many of the same products, such as stocks, at almost identical prices, irrespective of where the initial order originates.

There is a long history of best practices and regulation in the brokerage world. For instance, customer accounts should be segregated from the firm account, which isolates them from any financial problems at the brokerage firm. The collapse of Lehman Brothers is a good example, where brokerage customers were not impacted by the brokerage firm's default and had almost immediate access to their stocks and bonds. All brokerage accounts are also insured by the Securities Investors Protection Corporation (SIPC) that covers their assets when they have been misappropriated, usually through theft or fraud by the brokerage firm. This insurance has to return the full value of portfolio assets to the investor if they are within the SIPC guidelines.

What's Different in Trading Crypto Assets

While all of these protections and processes are often taken for granted for traditional financial investments they cannot be overlooked when choosing a crypto marketplace. Firstly, investors must realize that a crypto exchange is like the stock market. When you trade on a crypto exchange, you are taking the other side against counterparties at that specific exchange at the prevailing prices for the chosen exchange. Crypto exchanges have not yet developed efficient trading linkages the way traditional stock markets have. For stocks, when prices vary across exchanges, this creates an arbitrage opportunity where you could buy a stock at the cheaper exchange and simultaneously sell it at the more expensive venue. This would quickly close the gap and the differences in prices for the same asset would disappear.

That is not yet true for crypto exchanges, where the prevailing market prices for the same asset, say Bitcoin, could vary by several percentage points, which is not an insignificant amount of money when valuations are high. The differences are largely driven by varying liquidity across exchanges with the larger platforms offering better price discovery as a result of greater activity. At the moment, the top five exchanges for Bitcoin volume are bitfinex, bitflyer, bitstamp, Coinbase, and kraken, although these lists change often.

Given the borderless nature of crypto currencies, it is no surprise that the top five exchange listings have addresses in four different countries. Investors should assume that most exchanges are only lightly regulated, so picking the correct domicile is another important decision. While we have listed the largest exchanges there are countless other smaller exchanges that will tout lower fees, more innovate pricing, better trading opportunities, or any number of benefits. However, if these exchanges are not located in your country of residence, it may be difficult to resolve serious problems, such as hacking, which has proven to be an ongoing concern.

Foreign exchange of fiat currencies also poses a possible problem in crypto currency exchanges. While it may be anathema to consider cashing out into old paper money, there are still not many landlords that will take crypto for rent payments. Getting your crypto gains in your home currency may not be as simple if the exchange is located in a foreign jurisdiction and transacts mostly in non-domestic currency pairs. The same is true in setting up an account, with each exchange establishing its own funding requirements. For instance, Coinbase will accept credit cards, which many other exchanges will not. Others, including bitfinex until recently, only accepted coin deposits, so new traders would first need to acquire crypto from another exchange and transfer those coins to their account.

When working out the jurisdictional issues, it is important to select an exchange that trades the crypto that you are interested in. While practically all exchanges will trade Bitcoin and Ethereum, it is not a given that newer digital currencies will be on all platforms. While Ripple posted the strongest gains in 2017, one of the largest exchanges, Coinbase, did not offer trading in it. Given that there seem to be dozens of new currencies added each month, picking the right exchange for your trading habits is essential.

The need for security is obvious after the numerous hacks that have impacted exchanges all over the world. Mt. Gox was the largest but that did not stop hackers from essentially pushing the company into bankruptcy. While Mt. Gox was early in the crypto life cycle, the same cannot be said for coincheck, which lost $500 million worth of coins in early 2018. There have been numerous smaller hacks, many of which resulted in exchange closure and investor losses. Since there is no SIPC insurance for crypto exchanges, finding a firm with a good reputation that keeps customer assets offline goes a long way to avoid being hacked. Many of the hacks have occurred with hot wallets, or coin depositories that are connected to the internet, making them vulnerable to attacks. Investors should ultimately take their coins offline and store them in cold wallets that are not connected to the internet and may be on a storage device that you carry with you.

Using Wall Street for Crypto Investing

There are additional ways to participate in crypto currency trading without owning digital coins directly. As mentioned, the CBOE and CME both offer Bitcoin futures, which has seen a steady increase in volumes, although small relative to other more established financial contracts for interest rates, equity indices, and gold. There are also a limited number of ETFs that hold various interests in actual coins or futures contracts. There are also new ETFs that invest in firms involved in blockchain technology, although their top holdings are in tech firms that have embraced the blockchains, such as Microsoft, Overstock, and NVIDIA. There will undoubtedly be more ETFs that will be introduced in the coming year as interest remains high in the crypto currency space. The advantage of these products is their ability to tap into existing brokerage accounts, although it should be noted that some brokers restrict access to these investments.

Governments Get Involved

The growing popularity of crypto currencies is eliciting increasing responses from governments around the globe. One of the most appealing aspects of crypto is the borderless, anonymous aspects of its transactions. One of the early adopters of Bitcoin proved to be organized crime as well as its use for payments of illegal activities. While the commercial aspects of crypto have evolved significantly since those early years, there are varying estimates that a large portion of transactions continues to be driven by illicit activities, which governments will be keen to crack down.

At the other end of the spectrum is government's possible interest in getting into the crypto game. In its purest form, a fully functioning decentralized digital currency poses a significant risk to any government. As the previous chapters indicated, one of the most powerful weapons a government has is its ability to print money and declare it legal tender. When most of the world moved to fiat currencies, governments could essentially print money at will, which at times had disastrous results. The wide adoption of a digital currency outside of government intervention would be a major shift in power, which many feel will not be allowed to occur unfettered. One possible solution to this is the introduction of crypto currencies by governments themselves. The US, Russia, Japan, Sweden, Canada, Venezuela, and Estonia are just some of the countries that are analyzing the creation of government-sponsored crypto currencies.

Regulations Emerge and Are Often Welcome

There are therefore numerous reasons why governments would want to regulate crypto currencies and numerous avenues that they can pursue these regulations. Since Bitcoin is the most established of the alt-currencies, governments often frame their comments and actions with regard to Bitcoin, although their positioning will likely apply to all crypto currencies. Crypto is maturing quickly and gaining the attention of regulators as was clearly evident when the topic of regulation was discussed at a G-20 meeting of finance ministers in 2018.

Whether regulation provides greater legitimacy and therefore wider adoption of crypto currencies is to be seen, although greater government scrutiny seems inevitable. At the moment, only two countries, Japan and Switzerland, have deemed Bitcoin as legal tender, while many others, including the US, the European Union, the UK, and China, have explicitly stated that Bitcoin is not a legal tender.

Regulation has been focused on three phases of the crypto value chain: creation, trading, and usage. The rapid rise of alt-currencies outside of the major established names increased exponentially in 2017. New coins are often sold via an initial coin offering (ICO), with Bitcoin and Ethereum the predominant funding currencies. As recently as 2014, Ethereum was considered the most successful offering, having raised $18 million in Bitcoins during its ICO. Fast forward a few years and ICODATA reports that $90 million was raised by 29 ICOs in 2016, a fairly decent growth curve. However, all this pales in comparison to the $6 billion that was raised in 2017 through 800+ ICOs. This mania continues into 2018, which has exceeded 2017 totals, although new sales have slowed significantly since prices have collapsed.

While it will be challenging enough for most legitimate crypto offerings to succeed, scattered within the numerous offerings are fake and scam offerings. Concerns over fake ICOs have grown to the point that the Securities and Exchange Commission (SEC) set up a fake ICO to prove its point. This is prompting the regulation of ICOs as a security as bogus offerings become more common. While most of the world's government's continues to view ICOs with a skeptical eye, only the US, Canada, Taiwan, China, and South Korea have taken a definitive approach to either regulate them (in the case of the first three countries) or outright ban them, as in the case of China and South Korea.

Another area of regulation focuses on the exchanges that act as the main trading venues for crypto currencies. While the blockchain is viewed as unhackable, the same cannot be said for exchanges, which are often the repositories for the traded currencies. Hackers have successfully broken into numerous exchanges and stolen over $1 billion of crypto assets.

While it appears that any digital network is hackable these days, governments are at least discussing how to make exchanges more secure. Japan has been at the forefront of many crypto issues and their approach has been to regulate exchanges as some of the most notable hacking of exchanges occurred at companies operating under their jurisdiction. In contrast, China has become one of the most aggressive countries in limiting financial speculation around crypto currencies. It first banned ICOs and then subsequently cracked down on local exchanges, essentially requiring that they halt trading.

In the US the SEC has also become increasingly active in the crypto space, taking the approach that an ICO is like an initial public offering (IPO) and therefore subject to securities regulation. This would potentially make coins sold via an ICO a regulated security, in a vein similar to a regulated publically traded stock. Another recent example of greater government intervention is a report that the US Department of Justice is investigating possible market manipulation by traders in the crypto space.

Potentially one of the widest reaching discussions is a government's ability to outright ban the use of crypto. These discussions are often framed around the need to stop illegal activities, money laundering, and tax evasion. Undoubtedly, fears over the loss of control over a country's fiat currency system is likely equally concerning. As has been the case with government involvement in the crypto space, discussion is often slow to develop and regulations may be misplaced. For instance, the Internal Revenue Service (IRS) views crypto as property, and, as such, gains must be reported on income tax filings. That would essentially require a capital gains payment if crypto was used to make a purchase.

The IRS also recently requested user information from San Francisco-based Coinbase, one of the largest crypto exchanges. After initially resisting the IRS request, Coinbase was forced to comply after a Federal Court ruling. Coinbase will therefore turn over information on 14,000 users as the IRS attempts to collect unpaid taxes on crypto trading gains. While most countries continue to allow crypto as a payment mechanism, China and Zimbabwe presently do not allow crypto payments. The political nature of these actions is evident, however, as China is considered one of the more aggressive countries in wanting to establish its own centralized digital currency, while Zimbabwe is struggling with crippling hyperinflation. On a more practical level, payments regulation is questionable given the decentralized and anonymous nature of the blockchain. That will not stop further regulatory forays as the adoption of crypto currencies continues, although regulation may slow its expansion.

ICOs: Crypto Currencies' Hottest Trend

Special mention needs to be made about the ICO, as it emerged as one of the hottest trends in the crypto world in 2017. We will begin with the caveats, as these investments are highly speculative and increasingly subject to regulation and/or outright banning in certain countries. Recent data indicates that almost 50% of the ICOs floated in 2017 have already failed, taking with them $100 million in invested capital. To be sure, the ICOs that did not reach their first anniversary were on the fringe, as the amount raised is a small portion of the over $5 billion raised in 2017.

Another caveat has been the proliferation of outright ICO scams. Going by various names and offering various degrees of sophistication, some scams are as blatant as creating a fund-raising website, copying another venture's white paper, and waiting for the funds to be sent to the scammers. Many of these scams are shut down quickly and the amounts raised are not overly large, which does little to assuage those that lost money. There have been, nonetheless, large scams, such as the Pincon and iFan, which appears to be a Ponzi scheme that was able to raise $660 million from 32,000 people before collapsing. In that instance, there were apparently offices in Vietnam that claimed operations in Singapore and Dubai, a truly global effort.

The pure audacity of some of these scams is ultimately a by-product of the borderless and lightly regulated nature of the crypto sphere. Before we get into some of the investing aspects of ICOs, it is worth understanding how capital is raised in the traditional capital markets and how the process may be similar or different from an ICO. We will start with the distinction between venture capital (VC) funding and raising capital via an IPO. While there are no hard and fast rules on what type of company falls into the IPO versus VC buckets, there are various stages in a company's development that makes it better suited for one over the other.

ICOs are most often compared with IPOs, although we find that ICOs often have characteristics that intersect crowdsourcing, venture capital, and IPOs. An IPO is used to raise capital for a company and/or allow the owners of the private company to monetize their investment. A traditional company that is in the process of an IPO generally has been in business long enough for investors to attempt to place a valuation on the company. It is uncommon although not completely restricted for a startup to raise capital via an IPO. The age of an IPO company could be as short as a year to as long as decades. Revenues may therefore be near non-existent or already running into the billions. A successful IPO will be one where the company can get potential investors excited by the prospects of the business as a public entity.

IPOs sold to US investors are handled by registered brokers and there are very strict rules on what can be said and committed during the various stages of the offering. The SEC is involved in all US-based IPOs and the offering cannot move forward until the SEC declares the registration statement effective. At that point, the underwriters can begin taking orders and start the process of determining the initial offering price for the stock. The geographic distinction is important, as the SEC has no jurisdiction over international stock offerings unless they are listed on a US exchange. There are numerous international firms that jointly list their stock in their home market, as well as in the US, which opens their shareholder base to the much larger US equity markets.

In contrast, venture capital is a private investment in a company. While not always the case, if a company is in the early stage of its life cycle, it may only have access to venture capital to fund operations. Within the VC world, there are capital pools that are geared toward early state investing, while others look to fund more established but still evolving business models. The earliest stages of investment often involve angel investors, who provide funding for concepts or very early stage businesses. The risk of early stage investing is clearly greater, so these VC investors demand a greater portion of the company in order to provide funding. Crowdsourcing is another avenue in the venture funding continuum, where entrepreneurs/companies seek to raise funds from a wide group of investors. Generally, venture capitalists will always have an eye on a monetizing event, where they sell their shares of an investment via an IPO or merger, hopefully at higher valuations.

It is worth pointing out that VC investors are often investment professionals that manage pools of capital for institutional investors. As such, these professional investors have a multitude of tools and relationships to evaluate startup businesses and establish the value of targeted investments. IPOs are sold to a much larger audience, and the SEC's role is to ensure that ample information is available to prospective investors. Once an IPO is completed, public companies need to comply with ongoing reporting rules, while investment banking firms and other analysts often provide their opinions on company performance. The current valuation of a public company can be determined continuously via its stock price, while the value of VC investments depends on the most recent round of funding.

Based on the above description, ICOs often share properties of both VC companies and IPOs. Since many ICOs are at the concept stage, they share many of the risks associated with an early stage VC investment. Once successfully launched, an ICO is free to trade on a crypto exchange, and therefore shares similar aspects with an IPO. A constant for VC, IPO, and ICO investing is the need to thoroughly evaluate the business idea and trust the management team that is expected to make the offering a success.

While the risks are high, ICOs offer a revolutionary approach to fund-raising. In fact, various measures of tech startup funding via the VC channel now trail amounts raised via the ICO route. Distinctions are further blurred as traditional VC channels are now investing in crypto currency ventures with the intention of monetizing their investments via an ICO. All of this points to the continuation of ICOs for investors to evaluate and potentially participate. There are many common features for successful ICOs, beginning with a good idea, well-prepared white paper, strong management and technology team, and broad interest in the idea from both the technology and crypto communities. Since there is no lack of new applications, investors are likely to find projects where they can be a stakeholder, and hopefully use tokens as a participant in the network, or simply speculate on the appreciation of the tokens. It should be noted that the large influx of capital into the ICO arena has been around speculation recently, which has drawn increased scams and greater regulatory scrutiny. All in all, however, the potential of blockchain-driven applications and flexible fund-raising will further expand the ICO marketplace in 2018 and beyond.

Bibliography

CoinMarketCap, https://coinmarketcap.com/, Accessed 18 March 2018
Bloomberg, https://www.bloomberg.com, Accessed 18 August 2018
American Bullion, https://Americanbullion.com, Accessed 14 March 2018

O'Brian, Shaun, 2017, Understanding Consumer Cash Use: Preliminary Findings from the 2016 Diary of Consumer Payment Choice. Federal Reserve Bank of San Francisco

CNBC, Your guide to cryptocurrency regulations around the world and where they are headed, https://www.cnbc.com/2018/03/27/a-complete-guide-to-cyprocurrency-regulations-around-the-world.html, Accessed 30 April 2018

The Telegraph, The history of money: from barter to bitcoin, https://www.telegraph.co.uk/finance/businessclub/money/11174013/The-history-of-money-from-barter-to-bitcoin.html, Accessed 28 April 2018

National Bank of Belgium, Cowry Shells, a trade currency, https://www.nbbmuseum.be/en/2007/01/cowry-shells.htm, Accessed 12 April 2018

The Perfect Currency, History of Money, http://www.theperfectcurrency.org/main-history-of-money/history-of-money, Accessed 30 March 2018

The Balance, History of the Gold Standard, https://www.thebalance.com/what-is-the-history-of-the-gold-standard-3306136, Accessed 30 March 2018

Elwell, Craig K., 2011, Brief History of the Gold Standard in the United States, Congressional Research Services

Mishkin, Frederic S., The Economics of Money, Banking, and financial Markets, 11th edition

Bank of England, Our History, https://www.bankofengland.co.uk/about/history, Accessed 14 March 2018

Crabbe, Leland, 1989, The International Gold Standard and U.S. Monetary Policy from World War I to the New Deal, Federal Reserve Bank of St. Louis

Forbes, The 1870 – 1914 Gold Standard: the Most Perfect One Ever Created, https://www.forbes.com/sites/nathanlewis/2013/01/03/the-1870-1914-gold-standard-the-most-perfect-one-ever-created/#41cfaa6b4a6a, Accessed 15 March 2018

Selgin, George, 2013, The Rise and Fall of the Gold Standard in the United States, Cato Institute

Federal Reserve History, Creation of the Bretton Woods System, https://www.federalreservehistory.org/essays/bretton_woods_created, Accessed 12 April 2018

Bardo, Michael, 1993, The Gold Standard, Bretton Woods and other Monetary Regimes: An Historical Appraisal

Block Geeks, What is Cryptocurrency: Everything You Need to Know, https://blockgeeks.com/guides/what-is-cryptocurrency/, Accessed 5 May 2018

The Telegraph, A decade of cryptocurrency: from bitcoin to mining chips, https://www.telegraph.co.uk/technology/digital-money/the-history-of-cryptocurrency/, Accessed 5 May 2018

Cruz, Heather, Huang, Peter X., Levi, Stuart D., Dzierniejko, Ryan J., 2017, Blockchain Update, China Shuts down ICO Market, Skadden, Arps, Slate, Meagher & Flom, LLP

Obie, Stephen J., Rasmussen, Mark W., 2018, How Regulation Could Help Cryptocurrencies Grow, Harvard Business Review

Bitcoin Magazine, Cryptocurrency Regulations in 2018: Where the World Stands Right Now, https://bitcoinmagazine.com/articles/cryptocurrency-regulation-2018-where-world-stands-right-now/, Accessed 7 May 2018

Financial Times, Watchdogs tighten their grip on cryptocurrency exchanges, https://www.ft.com/content/41326d54-2381-11e8-add1-0e8958b189ea, Accessed 7 May 2018

Store of Value, List of High Profile Cryptocurrency Hacks So Far, http://storeofvalue-blog.com/posts/cryptocurrency-hacks-so-far-august-24th, Accessed 7 May 2018

Blockonomi, The History of the Mt Gox Hack: Bitcoin's Biggest Heist, https://blockonomi.com/mt-gox-hack, Accessed 7 May 2018

4

Crypto Currency: What Do We Know About Investment Performance and Risk?

Steven J. Shapiro

Introduction

Crypto currency originated in Nakamoto (2008), which described a digital payment system that did not require a third party, but instead a network of participants. The underlying technology, known as blockchain, has allowed for the growth of crypto currency. Bitcoin and more recently other crypto currencies serve as tokens used in blockchain systems.

Although Bitcoin has been traded 24 hours per day, 7 days per week, since 2010, rival crypto currencies started to appear in 2014. Since 2015, there have been competing coins, including Ethereum, which operates on the Ethereum network. Ethereum has a current market capitalization of $47.8 billion as of July 24, 2018, which is exceeded only by Bitcoin's $140.1 billion market capitalization on July 24, 2018.[1] Ethereum coins, like Bitcoins, are created through a mining network. However, Ethereum's network operates independently of Bitcoin's blockchain. To pay other computers on the network to complete tasks, Ethereum is used as the payment mechanism.

Ethereum is becoming important as it is designed to execute contracts that involve complicated financial transactions. A traditional financial transaction, such as settling a stock option or futures contract, involves two parties utilizing a third party, such as an organized financial exchange or a bank (for over-the-counter transactions) to conduct the transaction. However, in the traditional financial transaction, the two parties are paying fees to that third party.

[1] These statistics were obtained from https://www.cryptocompare.com on July 24, 2018, at 10:59 AM EDT.

S. Swammy et al., *Crypto Uncovered*, https://doi.org/10.1007/978-3-030-00135-3_4

Ethereum views itself as a mechanism through which the two parties can engage in transactions on a shared network with reduced transactions costs, no restrictions placed by third-party middlemen, and completely security.[2] The Ethereum network with its promise of decentralized smart contracts has become of interest for established information technology and financial services firms, such as J.P. Morgan Chase[3] and IBM,[4] which are interested in using blockchain networks as alternatives to traditional financial exchanges and banks acting as middlemen. In 2017, the non-profit Ethereum Enterprise Alliance was established to bring large companies, representatives of academia, and technology companies to build on Ethereum's smart contract blockchain technology.[5]

In addition to Ethereum, other coins have appeared over the last three years because of "initial coin offerings." For a startup, coin offerings are an alternative to funding via issuing stock or through venture capital financing. In effect, programmers raise money by creating and selling their own crypto currency that uses a framework like Bitcoin. Typically, the newly issued coins can only be used on a computing platform that the issuers are building.

Table 4.1 displays a ranking of market capitalizations of crypto currencies that have market capitalizations of at least $1 billion. As of July 24, 2018, 20 crypto currencies met this criterion.[6]

Over the remainder of this chapter, we survey prior literature on crypto currency pricing and returns; compare Bitcoin returns and risks with established financial assets; and compare returns and risk of alternative crypto currencies. We also discuss the implications of the establishment of crypto currency exchange-traded funds, as well as options and future contracts with crypto currency as the underlying financial asset. Finally, we conclude with suggested directions in future research.

Prior Empirical Literature on Crypto Currency Pricing and Returns

Since 2015, there has been an extensive literature on crypto currency pricing and returns. This research has focused on whether Bitcoin and other crypto currencies can serve as a hedge against other more established financial assets,

[2] https://www.ethereum.org

[3] J.P. Morgan calls Quorum an "enterprise-focused" version of Ethereum. https://www.jpmorgan.com/global/Quorum

[4] https://www.ibm.com/blockchain/

[5] https://entethalliance.org

[6] As of July 24, 2018, at 10:59 AM EDT per data obtained from https://www.cryptocompare.com

Table 4.1 Crypto currencies with market capitalization of $1 billion or greater as of July 24, 2018, 10:59 AM, EST

Rank	Coin	Market capitalization ($ billion)
1	Bitcoin	140.1
2	Ethereum	47.7
3	Ripple	17.6
4	Bitcoin Cash	14.6
5	EOS	8.4
6	Stellar	5.6
7	Litecoin	5.0
8	Cardano	4.5
9	Tronix	3.7
10	Iota	2.7
11	Tether	2.5
12	Binance Coin	2.3
13	Monero	2.3
14	Neo	2.2
15	Dash	2.1
16	Project Pai	2.0
17	Ethereum Classic	1.7
18	Huobi Token	1.7
19	NEM	1.6
20	0x	1.1

Source: www.cryptocompare.com, accessed July 24, 2018, 10:59 AM

such as stocks and foreign currency. In addition, financial researchers have focused on whether Bitcoin and other crypto currency assets are characterized by efficiency, that is, whether the prices of the asset reflect all relevant information.

Dyhrberg (2016) demonstrated that Bitcoin can be a hedge against the stock market and the US dollar, which makes Bitcoin extremely useful for portfolio diversification. Urquhart (2016) suggests that the Bitcoin market is inefficient but started moving toward efficiency from August 1, 2013, to and July 31, 2016. Nadarajah and Chu (2017) also show that the Bitcoin market is not efficient. Alvarez-Ramirez et al. (2018) found periods of efficiency that were followed by periods of inefficiency in the Bitcoin market.

Cheah and Fry (2016) show that over the period from July 2010 to November 2013, Bitcoin exhibited speculative bubbles and that speculative bubbles are a major component of Bitcoin prices. Hence, Cheah and Fry suggest that the fundamental value of Bitcoin is zero.

Bouri et al. (2017) demonstrate that Bitcoin is a hedge against economic uncertainty, as measured by the volatility indexes of 14 developing and developing world stock markets. Corbett et al. (2018) find evidence of price and volatility linkages between the crypto currencies Bitcoin, Ripple, and litecoin. However, the price and volatility of the three crypto currencies are unrelated to bond, gold, foreign exchange, and stocks markets. Demir et al. (2018) show that Bitcoin returns are positively related to economic policy uncertainty.

Lastly, Griffin and Shams (2018) and Gandal et al. (2017) investigate trading activity in Bitcoin. Gandal et al. investigated trading on the Mt. Gox Bitcoin Exchange between February and November 2013 and found two distinct periods in which approximately 600,000 Bitcoins (BTCs) valued at $188 million were acquired by agents who did not pay for the Bitcoins. During the second period, the USD-BTC exchange rate rose by an average of $20 at Mt. Gox on days when suspicious trades took place, compared to a slight decline on days without suspicious activity. Gandal et al. conclude that the suspicious trading activity caused Bitcoin to jump from around $150 to more than $1000 in two months.

Griffin and Shams used algorithms to analyze crypto currency data and found that purchases with Tether, a crypto currency backed by dollar reserves, are timed following market downturns and result in sizable increases in Bitcoin prices. Less than 1% of hours with heavy Tether transactions are associated with 50% of the meteoric rise in Bitcoin and 64% of the rise of other top crypto currencies. They argue that Tether is used to provide price support and manipulate crypto currency prices.

Bitcoin Returns and Risks Relative to Established Financial Assets

We compare Bitcoin returns and risks, as expressed by the volatility of returns, with the returns and risk of stocks, bonds, and gold. First, we examine Bitcoin.

Bitcoin's daily close prices were obtained from CryptoCompare, www.cryptocompare.com, for the period from July 19, 2010, through June 29, 2018. Figure 4.1 displays a plot of Bitcoin daily close prices over time. Figure 4.2 displays a plot of Bitcoin logarithmic daily returns. Note the large spike in the volatility of the daily returns in early 2014, which reflects Mt. Gox Exchange's problems at that time. Note that Mt. Gox handled nearly 70% of all trades in early 2014.

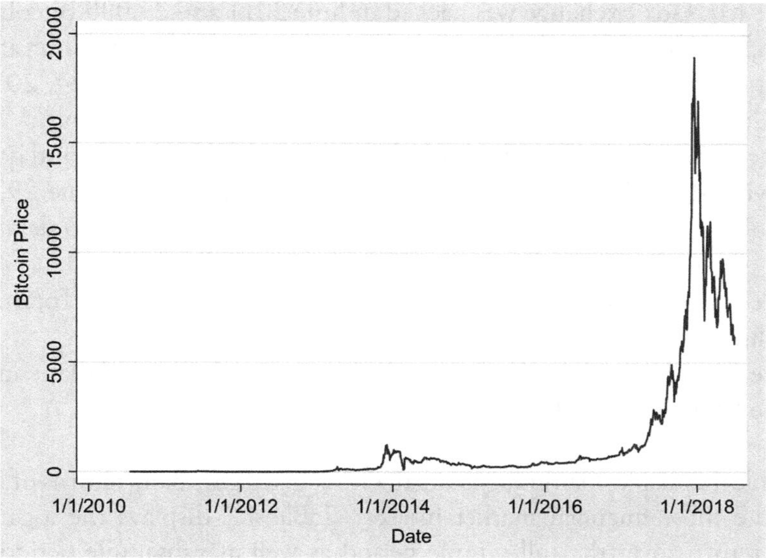

Fig. 4.1 Bitcoin daily closing price, July 19, 2010, through June 29, 2018

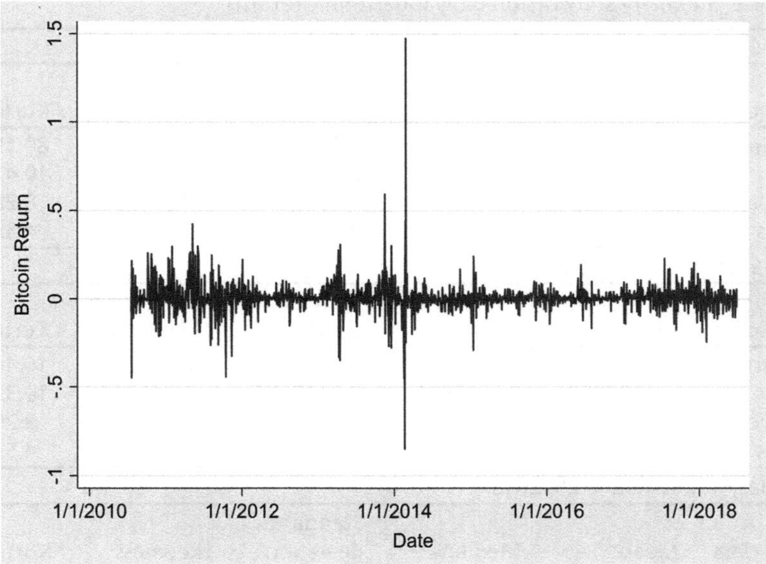

Fig. 4.2 Bitcoin daily logarithmic returns, July 19, 2010, through June 29, 2018

The Mt. Gox Exchange was hacked in June 2011 and 25,000 Bitcoins were stolen.[7] Bitcoin's price dropped from $17.50 to $0.01 in one hour after the stolen coins were then dumped on the market. On February 24, 2014, the Mt. Gox site was shut down after 850,000 Bitcoins went "missing."[8]

To compare Bitcoin returns with the returns of stocks, bonds, and gold, the following daily data over the period from July 19, 2010, to June 29, 2018, were obtained from the Federal Reserve Bank of St. Louis FRED database:

- The Bank of America Merrill Lynch US Corporate Master Total Return Value Index;
- The Gold Fixing Price in Dollars in the London Bullion Market; and
- The Wilshire 5000 Total Return Index.

Table 4.2 displays summary statistics for logarithmic daily returns of Bitcoin and the three financial market indexes. Table 4.2 displays the logarithmic daily returns over the full sample period as well as subsample periods from July 19, 2010, to January 31, 2014, and February 1, 2014, through June 29,

Table 4.2 Summary statistics on daily logarithmic returns

July 19, 2010–June 29, 2018					
Asset class	Mean	Median	Standard deviation	Skewness	Kurtosis
Bitcoin	0.0054952	0.0021542	0.0770317	2.783746	80.15076
Gold	−0.0000672	0.0001341	0.0098664	−0.7379136	10.47102
Equities	0.0005398	0.0007128	0.0092757	−0.5682937	8.285075
Bonds	0.0001636	0.0003162	0.0026274	−0.405708	4.525791
July 19, 2010–January 31, 2014					
Asset class	Mean	Median	Standard deviation	Skewness	Kurtosis
Bitcoin	0.0102524	0.0036697	0.0828311	0.1327075	10.44171
Gold	−0.0000531	0.0006971	0.0118165	−1.040465	10.33724
Equities	0.0006647	0.0008644	0.0106603	−0.5213826	8.269166
Bonds	0.0002164	0.0003948	0.0029071	−0.4718331	4.539512
February 1, 2014–June 29, 2018					
Asset class	Mean	Median	Standard deviation	Skewness	Kurtosis
Bitcoin	0.0016651	0.0018637	0.0051599	5.984047	177.8209
Gold	−0.0000786	−0.0001889	0.0079671	0.1921139	4.302291
Equities	0.0004399	0.0006334	0.0080014	−0.6376245	6.1505
Bonds	0.0001211	0.0002349	0.0023789	−0.3206363	4.051528

[7] The Mt. Gox Exchange was the largest exchange for trading Bitcoin in June 2011. This discussion is taken from Harvey (2016).

[8] See Vigna (2014) for a discussion of the problems of the Mt. Gox Exchange in early 2014.

Table 4.3 Correlations between daily logarithmic returns: Bitcoin, equity, bonds, and gold, July 19, 2010–June 29, 2018

	Bitcoin	Equity	Bonds	Gold
Bitcoin	1.0000			
Equity	0.0389	1.0000		
Bonds	−0.0062	−0.3181	1.0000	
Gold	0.0504	0.0155	0.0459	1.0000

2018. For both the overall sample and the subsample periods, the mean and median return statistics indicate that Bitcoin outperformed stocks, gold, and bonds. The standard deviation in logarithmic daily returns was substantially higher than the standard deviation in logarithmic daily returns for stocks, gold, and bonds. Although higher average daily returns could be earned holding Bitcoin, relative to the other asset classes, the risk was substantially higher.

Table 4.3 displays correlations between the daily logarithmic returns of Bitcoin, stocks, gold, and bonds over the full sample period. As is apparent from the low correlations between Bitcoin and the three asset classes, not only is Bitcoin more volatile than the other asset classes, but its daily returns are not closely related to the returns of the other asset classes. Table 4.3 is consistent with the literature reviewed in section "Bitcoin Returns and Risks Relative to Established Financial Assets" of this chapter as the low correlations of Bitcoin returns with other assets confirms that the addition of Bitcoin to a portfolio that contains conventional financial assets can provide the benefits of further diversification.

Comparative Financial Performance of Alternative Crypto Currencies

To compare the financial performance of alternative crypto currencies, a sample of crypto currencies was drawn from crypto currencies with market capitalizations of $1 billion or more, as shown in Table 4.1. The final sample also included crypto currencies for which there was daily price data from August 7, 2015, through June 29, 2018. The final sample consisted of daily closing prices obtained from CryptoCompare, www.cryptocompare.com, for the following crypto currencies with ticker symbol in parentheses: Bitcoin (BTC), Ethereum (ETH), Ripple (XRP), and Litecoin (LTC).

Figures 4.3, 4.4, and 4.5 display line plots of BTC, ETH, XRP, and LTC prices over the sample period. Visual inspection of Figs. 4.3, 4.4, and 4.5, particularly as prices of the four crypto currencies began a rapid rise in 2017, suggests that the prices of the four crypto currencies moved together over time.

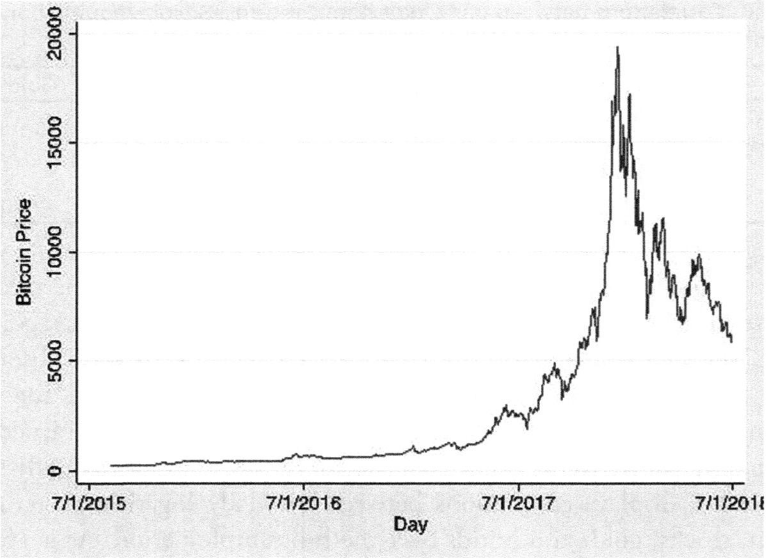

Fig. 4.3 Bitcoin price, August 7, 2015–June 29, 2018

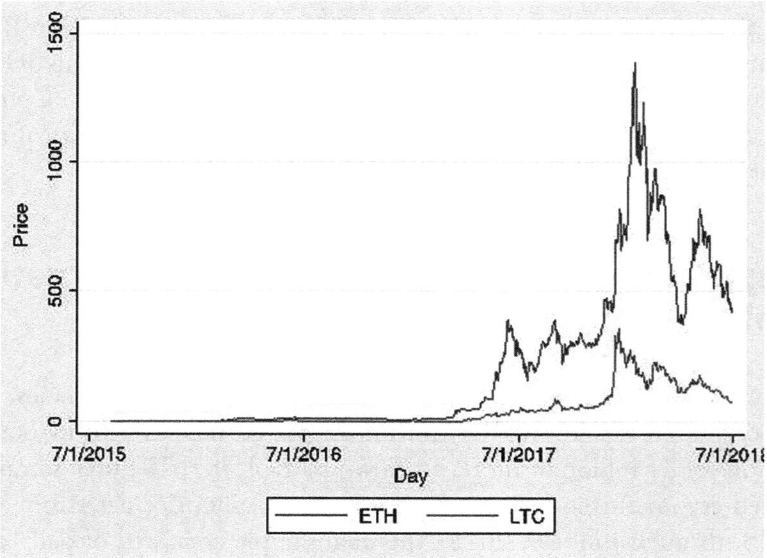

Fig. 4.4 Ethereum and Litecoin prices, August 7, 2015–June 29, 2018

The line plots in Fig. 4.6 are used to display relative performance data for each of the four crypto currencies The line plots in Fig. 4.6 consist of the transformation of the daily data for each data series where each data series' value is divided by that series' value on August 7, 2015. This allows us to examine how equal dollar investments in each crypto currency performed over the entire sam-

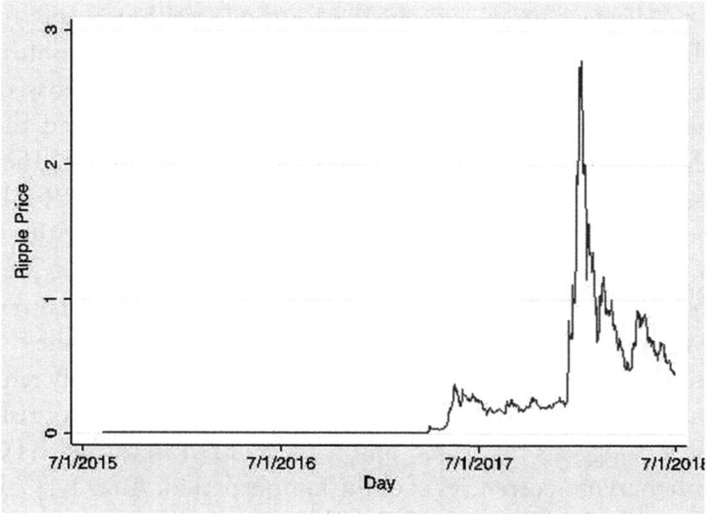

Fig. 4.5 Ripple price, August 7, 2015–June 29, 2018

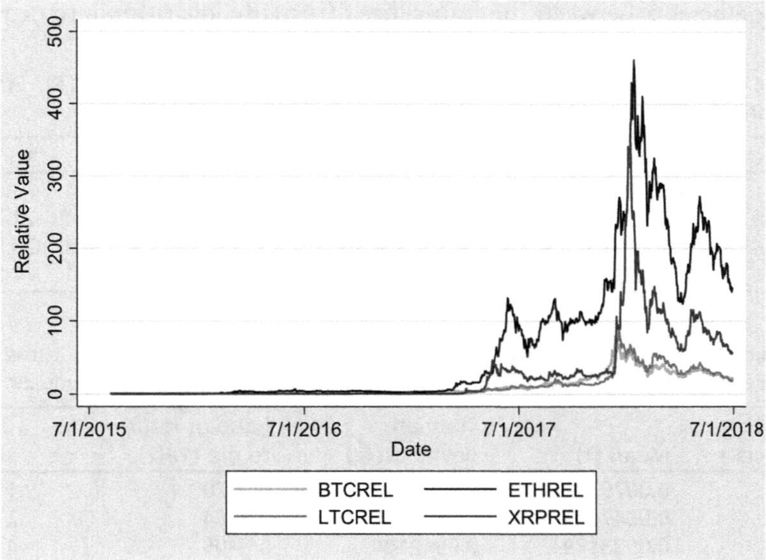

Fig. 4.6 Value of equal $1.00 investments in Bitcoin (BTC), Ethereum (ETH), Ripple (XRP), Litecoin (LTC), and cci30 Index, August 7, 2015–June 29, 2018

ple period. As shown in Fig. 4.6, even with price declines from their peak in early January 2018, crypto currencies have had rapid price appreciation over the entire sample period. From August 7, 2015, to June 29, 2018, $1.00 invested in ETH was worth $145.08 on June 29, 2018, and $1.00 invested in XRP was worth $56.63. A $1.00 invested in BTC was worth $22.32 on June 29, 2018, and $1.00 invested in LTC was worth $19.28 on June 29, 2018.

Table 4.4 displays summary statistics for the logarithmic daily returns for each of the crypto currencies. The mean and median returns confirm what is shown in line plots of Fig. 4.6 as a ranking of average returns based on both mean and median returns indicated that ETH and XRP had the highest average daily logarithmic returns and BTC and LTC the lowest. The standard deviations of daily logarithmic returns also suggested that XRP, followed by ETH, was the most volatile of the four crypto currencies over the August 7, 2015, to June 29, 2018, sample period. Higher average returns were associated with higher volatility in returns for the individual crypto currencies.

Table 4.5 ranks crypto currency performance by dividing the mean daily logarithmic return by the standard deviation of logarithmic daily returns. This allows for an examination of the average daily return per unit of risk (volatility). Table 4.5 suggests that based on the ratio of return to risk, BTC outperformed other crypto currencies over the sample period. After BTC, ETH was the highest ranked followed by LTC and XRP.

Pairwise correlations between the logarithmic daily returns of the four crypto currencies were examined. Table 4.6 displays Pearson pairwise correlation coefficients between the four series. The daily logarithmic returns of all

Table 4.4 Summary statistics on daily logarithmic returns: Bitcoin (BTC), Ethereum (ETH), Ripple (XRP), and Litecoin (LTC), August 7, 2015–June 29, 2018

Asset class	Mean	Median	Standard deviation	Skewness	Kurtosis
BTC	0.0029382	0.0029609	0.0408234	−0.207124	7.093563
ETH	0.0047089	0	0.0806132	−1.195264	21.22295
XRP	0.0038189	−0.0017861	0.0942104	1.860641	23.94807
LTC	0.0027994	0	0.0590146	1.775621	17.84802

Table 4.5 Ratio of average daily return to risk based on daily logarithmic returns: Bitcoin (BTC), Ethereum (ETH), Ripple (XRP), and Litecoin (LTC), August 7, 2015–June 29, 2018

Asset class	Mean (1)	Standard deviation (2)	Ratio of return to risk (1)/(2)	Ranking
BTC	0.0029382	0.0408234	0.0720	1
ETH	0.0047089	0.0806132	0.0584	2
XRP	0.0038189	0.0942104	0.0405	4
LTC	0.0027994	0.0590146	0.0474	3

Table 4.6 Correlations between daily logarithmic returns: Bitcoin (BTC), Ethereum (ETH), Ripple (XRP), and Litecoin (LTC), August 7, 2015–June 29, 2018

	BTC	ETH	LTC	XRP
BTC	1.0000			
ETH	0.3483	1.0000		
LTC	0.5698	0.3177	1.0000	
XRP	0.1912	0.1322	0.2380	1.0000

four crypto currencies are positively related to each other. The daily logarithmic returns of BTC and LTC have the strongest pairwise correlation among the four crypto currency returns. The weakest pairwise correlations are between XRP daily logarithmic returns and the logarithmic returns of the other three crypto currencies.

Establishment of Exchange-Traded Funds, Options, and Future Contracts on Crypto Currency

Bitcoin and other crypto currencies are still young and, as noted above, characterized by volatility in returns. However, investor interest in crypto currency is causing financial services firms to investigate the establishment of retail exchange-traded funds (ETFs) that contain crypto currency and exchange-traded options and future contracts with crypto currency as the underlying asset. These financial innovations revolving around crypto currencies have come under increased scrutiny of financial regulators, as well as brought new investor capital into crypto currency markets.

On March 3, 2017, the Securities and Exchange Commission (SEC) rejected an application by the Better Alternative Trading System (BATS) to offer the proposed Winklevoss Bitcoin Trust ETF, which would have allowed retail investors to buy Bitcoin in the manner that they purchase common stock (Weiczner 2017). The SEC expressed concerns about the potential for fraud and price manipulation. Despite the SEC's rejection of the BATS application, the Coinbase Exchange is planning to offer an ETF for retail customers that will be an index fund based on multiple crypto currencies once there is regulatory approval (Weiczner 2018). Bitwise has filed a proposal for an ETF that would track a portfolio of ten crypto currencies (Rooney 2018). Neither the Bitwise nor the Coinbase proposals had been approved by the EC at the time this book was published.

The LedgerX trading and clearinghouse platform received approval from the Commodity Futures Trading Commission (CFTC) to trade and clear swaps and options digital currency. Currently, LedgerX lists options and swaps on Bitcoin.[9] As of April 2018, LedgerX planned to expand by trading options and swaps on Ethereum.[10] In December 2017, the Cantor Exchange received

[9] https://ledgerx.com/about, accessed July 25, 2018.

[10] https://www.coindesk.com/ledgerx-sees-7x-jump-in-options-trading-6-months-after-launch/, accessed July 25, 2018.

CFTC approval to offer Bitcoin options contracts.[11] As of the time of publication of this volume, the Cantor Exchange had not begun trading of the Bitcoin options.

In December 2017, the Chicago Mercantile Exchange (CME) and the Chicago Board of Exchange (CBOE) received CFTC approval to trade Bitcoin futures contracts.[12] Both the CME and the CBOE are in the early stages of offering Bitcoin futures contracts.

Currently, regulated derivative contracts on crypto currency are in their infancy. As they become more established, they provide the promise of providing greater liquidity to trading of crypto currency.

Conclusions and Future Directions in Research

Bitcoin and other crypto currencies have had a short history to date. Although Bitcoin has outperformed conventional financial assets, the high returns have been accompanied by volatility.

As Bitcoin and other crypto currencies mature, along with associated derivative contracts, there is a need for empirical research. Future research needs include:

- Examination of whether the appearance of derivatives contracts on options are affecting the pricing and efficiency of trading in Bitcoin.
- The examination of the interrelationship of crypto currency pricing with traditional financial markets.
- Quantification of the degree to which prices of individual coins are affected by the pricing of other coins.

Bibliography

Alvarez-Ramirez, J., E. Rodriguez and C. Ibara-Valdez. 2018. "Long-Range Correlations and Asymmetry in the Bitcoin Market," *Physica A* 492: 948–966.

Bouri, Elie, Peter Molnr, Georges Azzi, David Roubaud and Lars Ivar Hagfors. 2017. "On the Hedge and Safe Haven Properties of Bitcoin: Is It Really More than a Diversifier?" *Finance Research Letters*, 20:192–198.

[11] United States Commodities Futures Trading Commission, https://www.cftc.gov/sites/default/files/idc/groups/public/%40customerprotection/documents/file/backgrounder_virtualcurrency01.pdf

[12] Ibid.

Cheah, Eng-Tuck and John Fry. 2016. "Speculative Bubbles in Bitcoin markets? An Empirical Investigation into the Fundamental Value of Bitcoin," *Economics Letters* 130: 32–36.

Corbett, Shaen, Andrew Meegan, Charles Larkin, Brian Lucey and Larisa Yarovaya. 2018. "Exploring the Dynamic Relationships between Cryptocurrencies and other Financial Assets," *Economics Letters*, forthcoming.

Demir, Ender, Giray Gozgor, Chi K.M. Lao and Samuel A. Vigne. 2018. "Does Economic Policy Uncertainty Predict the Bitcoin returns? An Empirical Investigation," *Finance Research Letters,* forthcoming.

Dyhrberg, Anne H. 2016. "Bitcoin, Gold and the Dollar – a GARCH Volatility Analysis," *Finance Research Letters* 16: 85–92.

Gandal, Neil, J.T. Hamrick, Tyler Moore and Tali Oberman. 2017. In *16th Workshop on the Economics of Information Security (WEIS).*

Griffin, John and Amin Shams. 2018. "Is Bitcoin Really Untethered?" https://papers.ssrn.com/sol3/papers.cfm?abstract_id=3195066.

Harvey, Campbell. 2016. "Cryptofinance," https://ssrn.com/abstract=243829.

Nadarajah, Saralees and Jeffrey, Chu. 2017. "On the Inefficiency of Bitcoin," *Economic Letters* 150: 6–9.

Nakamoto, Satoshi. 2008. "Bitcoin: A Peer-to-Peer Electronic Cash System," https://bitcoin.org/bitcoin.pdf.

Rooney, Kate. 2018. "Bitwise joins the race to launch SEC-regulated cryptocurrency ETF". https://www.cnbc.com/2018/07/24/bitwise-joins-the-race-to-launch-sec-regulated-cryptocurrency-etf.html.

Urquhart, Andrew. 2016. "The Inefficiency of Bitcoin," *Economics Letters* 148:80–82.

Vigna, Paul. 2014. "5 Things About Mt. Gox's Crisis". *The Wall Street Journal.* April 25.

Weiczner, Jennifer 2017. "What the SEC Bitcoin ETF Decision Means for the Future of Cryptocurrency". *Fortune* March 10. http://fortune.com/2017/03/10/bitcoin-price-etf-winklevoss-approval/.

Weiczner, Jennifer 2018. "Coinbase Eyes Bitcoin ETF With New Cryptocurrency Index Fund". *Fortune* March 6. http://fortune.com/2018/03/06/coinbase-bitcoin-cryptocurrency-fund/.

5

Managing the Crypto Marketplace

Sarah Swammy, Richard Thompson, and Marvin Loh

Entrepreneurs entering the crypto currency world will do so via an initial coin offering (ICO). ICOs in general have a community of users that participate in building a perceived value of the token or coin by using it as a medium of exchange for a given marketplace of goods or services provided by the ICO network—or trading the token or coin on a crypto currency exchange. Designing a system of governance for the community is the burden of entrepreneurs who dare to take on such an endeavor to ensure their fate is not the same as that of Ross Ulbricht. Participant management was not a topic of high interest for the original designers of digital currencies or Bitcoin. The works of the cypherpunks, the group associated with creating a body of works that became the foundation and inspiration for Bitcoin, do little to address the issue of participant management. In their search and quest for creating a payment system that was completely removed from any central banking system or authority, the task of verifying and managing the original identity authenticity of individuals was not the purpose of the technology. To perform such task would appear to go against the privacy ideals of the original founders of the technology. The issues, of primary focus for the original contributors, were solving how to maintain privacy and anonymity through encryption, proving authenticity of identity with the use of private and public keys, and eliminating double counting or counterfeiting. Other pressing issues for launching a decentralized payment system were having a mechanism that performed the service of a digital notary for proof of transaction and having an immutable and distributed database on a decentralized peer-to-peer network that acted as the official books of records.

The original contributors were able to accomplish this monumental task of a decentralized payment system with the remarkable collections of works of

S. Swammy et al., *Crypto Uncovered*, https://doi.org/10.1007/978-3-030-00135-3_5

cryptographers, mathematicians, and software engineers. This relatively small population of individuals of exceptional intelligence, and some with altruistic ideals of changing society, laid the foundation and created the tools to play the digital currency game. Bitcoin was the first crypto currency that became most popular and accepted by the general public, although there were other digital currency games before Bitcoin. Referring to crypto currency in the context of a game allows for the introduction of the concept of participant management, and creates a framework for an individual of non-technical background to understand the fundamental concept of digital currency in general.

Identifying the fundamental inner game within digital currencies or Bitcoin that is played continuously is the first step to understanding the essence of crypto currencies. It is very important to realize that miners race to solve a very difficult problem called the hash function. Twelve new Bitcoins are minted to the miner that solves the hash function. The miner can be an individual or a group of individuals that acts as a single entity. Twelve new Bitcoins will only be assigned to one wallet for the winner of the hash function. The general public would discover that playing the game is not as easy as it appears. The common question everyone would ask in the beginning period of Bitcoin, before Mt. Gox, the first exchange to come online to trade Bitcoin or crypto currencies, was "How do you get bitcoin?" Bitcoin was always present but not easily accessible for the general public with no computer training.

The original contributors who created the technologies that comprise the foundation of the Bitcoin.org network were focused on building rock-solid tools of the game and focused on who would play the game.

The task of becoming a legitimate currency is challenging for any crypto currency. To satisfy the fundamental requirements of being a medium of exchange and a store of value is not trivial. It is not obvious to the general public how any of the fundamental requirements are satisfied.

Early Days of Bitcoin

Let's look at the early days of Bitcoin to understand how a transaction was performed. Transactions were conducted through a command prompt. Using a command prompt to perform everyday transactions such as in store supermarket payments, paying for gas, or paying for a cup of coffee would be sheer torture. Therefore, getting enough traction by the general public to honestly want to use Bitcoin as a medium of exchange was unfathomable during those incubation years. However, there was very high interest among the contributors as they remained focused on the tools of the game, the cryptology, Merkle Trees for the distributed database, and the methods to reach a consensus.

During this period of making digital technology a currency there was little or no mention of implementing a framework to manage the conduct of and impose limits on the users of the tools.

There were not many participants playing the game outside of the software enthusiasts demonstrating the virtues of the technology and a relatively small number of speculators betting that a marketplace would come and bring in a wave of new participants.

Figure 5.1 represents the historical and forecasted number of Bitcoins in circulation. The projected shape of the curve shows that the number of Bitcoins in circulation will asymptotically approach 21 million. Combining this chart with the historical price chart provides a picture of the daily market value of Bitcoin which gives an indication of the number of participants. The daily market chart will show how Bitcoin is trending in becoming a currency. As more and more participants use it for a medium of exchange and avenues open up to facilitate access to digital coins, users see a pathway of how it could become categorized as a currency.

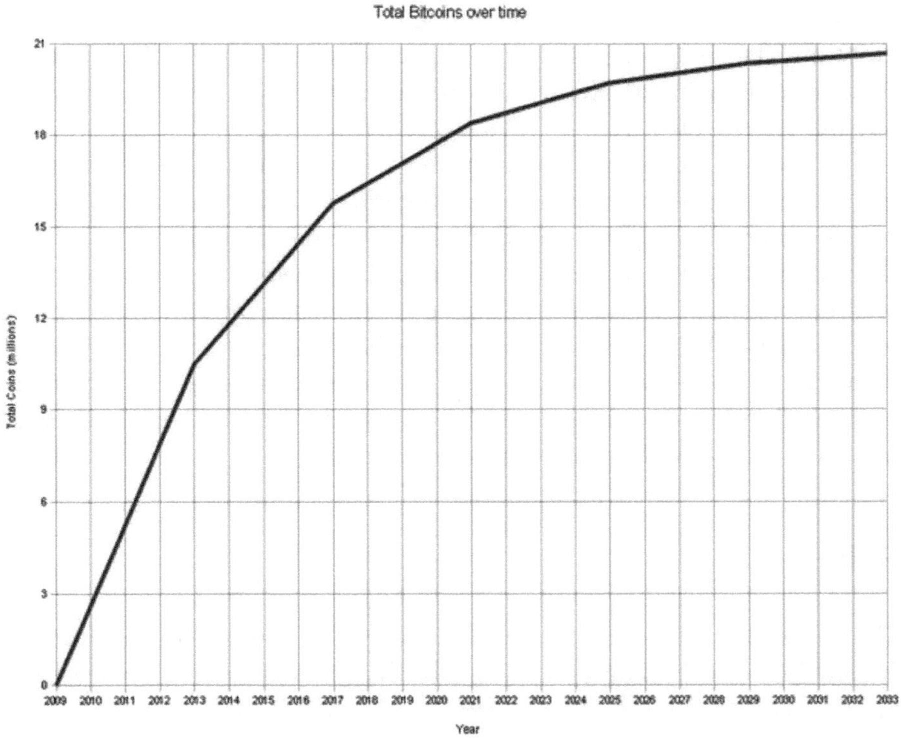

Fig. 5.1 Historical and forecasted number of Bitcoins in circulation

Establishing a Baseline Value for Bitcoin

Three events occurred within 18 months of the first transaction between Satoshi Nakamoto and Hal Finney that began the acceptance of the idea of Bitcoin becoming a feasible consumer currency. On October 5, 2009, New Liberty Standard assigns a value to Bitcoin based upon the cost of electricity used to generate or mine Bitcoin. They open a service to buy and sell Bitcoin for an exchange rate of 1309.03 BTC for $1. New Liberty Standard, at a minimum, created a baseline to establish the value of Bitcoin. The next event was a business-to-business fiat to Bitcoin transaction that occurred when New Liberty Standard bought 5050 BTC from Sirius for 5.02 using PayPal. The third event was a business-to-consumer transaction that occurred when a pizza was bought using jercos for 10,000 BTC valued at $25. This established the first concrete value of Bitcoin at $0.0025 per coin. Before those events the transactions were confined to the cult community of cypherpunks, software enthusiasts, and speculators who anticipated a new world blossoming out of the digital domains.

These events were necessary to create a pathway for Bitcoin to become recognized as legitimate currency by the public in general. The number of participants using the coin and playing the game was still rather low between 2009 and 2010 and the participants were confined mainly to software enthusiasts, special libertarian groups, and special interest groups such as the March on Wall Street crowd.

The need to incorporate a participant management system was very low because the number of individuals playing the game was relatively small. The central governments of the world have many more larger issues of concern than trying to put a governmental oversight over what would appear to be cult-like software enthusiasts wanting to make seemingly fictitious payments to one another. Who uses the coin and for what was of no interest to the originators of Bitcoin. Their concern was to make an instrument that could uniquely transfer value and be recorded across a decentralized network, ensuring that the tools of the game work as advertised.

Silk Road

The participation level can grow organically at a slow or fast rate with no expected time frame. However, Ross Ulbricht spikes the participant levels and has the network drinking from a firehose with Silk Road coming online. He brings the uncontrolled, unmanaged world of an open marketplace with no oversight to an intrinsically vetted marketplace of computer specialists and trading speculators.

Participation levels grew beyond organic growth with the e-commerce site of Silk Road being launched in February 2011 and bringing in a pool of participants that elevated the Bitcoin experiment from a game to an enterprise. By the time Gawker released their article about the infamous site, Bitcoin had spiked from a value of 0.97 just under a dollar to 9.21. That elevation in price corresponding with the current volume of Bitcoin in circulation at that time of 5.8 million equates to a market size of $53,481,000. Those levels of participants and market size most certainly drew the attention of the enforcement community and government authorities.

During the incubation year when Bitcoin was perceived by the legal community as an overambitious game played among a niche group for pennies, even as the circulation size grew with mining, the incentive value was still low with the monetary reward value of 50 Bitcoins valued under a penny each. The number of Bitcoins rewarded halves as Bitcoin circulation levels reach certain values. Currently Bitcoin is minted at 12.5 per transaction. The mining reward value incentives are much higher now than during the incubation period. Even during the time of the launch of Silk Road the reward mining incentive values was significant at approximately $50 per transaction. The number of Bitcoins rewarded halves approximately every four years; that is why the current number issued is 12.5 having gone through two rounds of halving from the initial 50. However, the price of a Bitcoin has spiked dramatically, having a monetary reward value over $100,000.00 per transaction.

Creating a Store of Value

During this period of Bitcoin the idea of it being a legitimate coin was a stretch when trying to determine how it was a store of value. The creators of the tools of Bitcoin came up with a mechanism to transfer value and a decentralized system to accurately record the historical transfer value. Determining what the value is, which is a very important issue in regard to being a store of value, is not the responsibility of those who created the tools. That responsibility became the task of speculators who began to use Bitcoin in the very early days after the original first transaction. The challenge is getting the masses to play the game. At this point although it may appear to be rather insignificant to institute a participant management framework, it is important to zero in on who is playing the game and lay out the components of the game.

First there is the Bitcoin network. Bitcoin.org houses the incredible technology that issues a new Bitcoin or mints a new coin through mining. The Bitcoin game is played by miners attempting to solve a very difficult problem called a hash function that is solved by finding the next node in the Merkle Tree by using the encrypted information of the previous node. Whoever solves the problem is awarded 12.5 new Bitcoins and the next transaction block. These miners act as the notary in the digital game. Let's take an inventory of who is playing the game at this point. They can safely be called the contributors of the game or creators of the game, the owners or administrators of bitcoin.org. That would be one group. The other group are the speculators. The last group are the miners.

During this time, it was still a niche game played only by a small community relative to the global population. There is an implied vetting process at this point of the game. Only individuals with the wherewithal and patience to actually build a Bitcoin client and use a command prompt to execute a series of commands that connected a digital wallet to a transaction and assigned a value to the number of units of currency they desired to buy or sell could play the game. This is a very sophisticated process to perform manually. The likelihood of the everyday consumer of goods and services using this as a medium of exchange is extremely low. The threat of digital currencies or Bitcoin challenging fiat currencies or the current monetary system is laughable. How would the masses accept transacting through a command prompt and determining their current balance by executing a series of commands through an archaic terminal. During the period of 2008 through 2010 the buzz created around Bitcoin among the niche groups playing the game for any central government would appear to be a waste of resources to put any effort to govern these small niche groups.

Even as the technology matured and the formal exchange of Mt. Gox came online to facilitate transactions in Bitcoin, the groups playing the game were still small relative to the global mass population. Speculators who were driving the price of and market for Bitcoin at that point had the price at around 0.01; with the pool of Bitcoin capping out at 21 million Bitcoins, the total market value of which at that time would have been $210,000.00. What incentive is there to participate in that game betting on a future marketplace that could potentially drive the price up to make it a legitimate store of value.

The Market Awakens

As crypto currencies gain traction to become an accepted medium of exchange for day-to-day transactions, entrepreneurs who are creating the business to drive these marketplaces are faced with the challenge of how to manage the onboarding of individuals into the marketplace that satisfies regulators and government officials, besides maintaining privacy concerns of participants that use the marketplace. It is evident from the lesson learned from Silk Road that marketplaces which incorporate a network exchange and digital payment system are the platform in which any digital currencies will become accepted as crypto currencies. From the fundamental basis of a currency being a medium of exchange and a store of value, it is not clear whether Bitcoin alone or any other crypto currency without the marketplace is a currency. It is not obvious that the currency is a store of value.

It is true that digital currencies are a payment and accounting system. The digital technology can transfer a unit value from one wallet to another and ensure that double counting and counterfeiting are not taking place. Satoshi Nakamoto's transferring 10 Bitcoins to Hal Finney as the first Bitcoin transaction demonstrated the success of a decentralized payment system and a primitive marketplace of the Bitcoin network. The obvious question to ask is what is the value of 10 Bitcoins. The accounting technology of the network is legitimate, but not the value system. Colonists used land as collateral to set the value of fiat currencies. This practice set a reference point or benchmark for the value of fiat currencies. And the benchmark evolved to the gold standard to the measure of creditworthiness of the country to which the fiat currency is assigned.

The values of Bitcoins and digital currency are not easy to determine based on a benchmark. Initially the benchmark was based upon speculation of a perceived marketplace coming up in which patrons would use the digital instrument of value as the medium of exchange for the marketplace. In the early days cult-like enthusiasts would perform the same task as Satoshi and use a command prompt on a computer after building a Bitcoin client to buy Bitcoins at an extremely low value. This assigning of value based upon speculation created a synthetic store of value for Bitcoin. In that sense it became a perceived currency due to the assigned speculative value and it was a proper means of exchange. From that scenario a primitive currency was created. Participant management at that stage of development of the currency was an overkill because only technology-driven cultish enthusiasts would use the currency. The general public was not going to carry their computer with them to the supermarket and use a command prompt to execute a Bitcoin transaction to buy a loaf of bread. At that stage of the evolution of digital currency there was no utility due to lack of mass acceptance. It was a challenge faced by crypto currency entrepreneurs to move the acceptance of digital currency from cult acceptance to mass appeal to becoming an icon-like fiat currency. The global markets understand the value and symbol of British pound, US dollar, French franc, and many other currencies that make up the G20.

Those countries that comprise the G20 have currencies that govern the marketplace of their countries that took decades to prove their creditworthiness and formalize their currency into a global symbol of value. How do digital currencies go through that same process to get that near-rock-solid perception of value that fiat currencies have achieved. One clear way as demonstrated by Silk Road is by creating a marketplace to drive transaction activity beyond the levels of cult user of the digital coin—create a marketplace that is inviting and design a user experience that is easy for the everyday user in terms of transaction Satisfying these two requirements creates a pathway for the coin to grow in value and helps in establishing a benchmark for the goods and services within the marketplace with a more concrete or defined metric as the object of value.

With the increase in the number of transactions and different types of users participating in the marketplace driving the value of the currency, there is the demand to institute a management system that governs the many types of users and how transactions are conducted. Even though the marketplace is not governed by a central authority, it does not mean the marketplace should go unregulated by a marketplace authority that brings the value-added services of delivering the platform.

As witnessed by the severe prosecution of Ross Ulbricht, owners of the marketplace will be held to standards of central bodies and associated legal repercussions. Does anyone get into business knowing they will go to jail? Not instituting a governance or participant management framework almost guarantees that outcome. The Silk Road case is an example that one needs to take heed of.

At the least a framework that is transparent as to how individuals or groups are onboarded into the network and also how they are categorized once inside the network is imperative.

With the increased pressure from law enforcement agencies backed by politicians to enforce anti-money laundering (AML) and know your customer (KYC) laws, it is imperative that any entrepreneur thinking of creating a business based upon digital currencies take heed of the precedent set by the judges' sentencing and ruling of the Silk Road case. Silk Road is a case study that highlights the importance of undertaking great caution when building a governance framework in the early stages of embarking on a crypto currency enterprise. The adoption of crypto currency, Silk Road has shown, will be through marketplace portals offering goods and services that drive user transaction activity.

The trading of the currency itself is a direct consequence of the transaction activity through the portal. As is evident from the details of the investigation done by the FBI in the case the owners of the marketplace are the direct target of the investigation. It is clear for anyone with a technology background that any viable digital currency enterprise is made up of three tightly integrated but separate networks which we will detail. However, the legal investigation only targets the owner of the marketplace hub. Investigating the details of the Silk Road scandal, which cast a very dark shadow over crypto and digital currencies, alludes to that fact. It is evident that Ross Ulbricht built a user-friendly marketplace utilizing the web where vendors of many different industries were able to post anything their imaginations could conceive of and patrons could buy goods and services of almost anything their minds could imagine. This ease and feasibility led to Mr. Ulbricht's downfall, given the lack of oversight or a mechanism of control to curb certain activities from taking place through the portal. The prosecutors and the judge targeted the owner of the site to the full extent of the law, with RICO-style legal frameworks to enforce maximum penalties.

This hardline stance by law enforcement was fueled by the cries of politicians such as Charles Schumer after an article published by Gawker in June 2011 brought greater awareness about the site. The egregious misuses of the site for illicit activity was too much for anyone to overlook as individuals involved in narcotic trafficking frequently used the site to coordinate drug deals.

The Silk Road website, which had a customer-friendly electronic storefront that displayed bricks of cocaine as deftly as Amazon displays books, was the cyber underworld's largest black market, with $1.2 billion in sales and nearly a million customers. This client experience may have led its participants to assume that the site could be a haven for illicit activity. Beyond illegal drugs, the site served as a bazar for fake passports, drivers' licenses, and other documents as well as a site for illegal service providers such as hit men, forgers, and computer hackers.

The lack of oversight and the ability to facilitate payments with very low fees made the Silk Road attractive and the promised land for many different types of entrepreneurs. This was not only used upstanding citizen, it also became a conduit for individuals who had criminal intent. This activity more than likely was not the intended purpose of Ross Ulbricht launching the site. However, with no governance for those who participated in the site he was found culpable.

The FBI and prosecutors were going to make Ross Ulbricht the fall guy. The case was tried in the Federal Court in Manhattan; although Ulbricht operated in San Francisco, he was not tried in California. The trial, which began on January 13, 2015, sent a strong message to the crypto world as it was tried in the financial capital of America and not in the jurisdiction where the alleged crime was committed. Establishing the identity of the owner of the site was key for prosecuting the case, in which law enforcement identified the owner as Ross Ulbricht. Ulbricht admitted to founding the Silk Road website, but claimed to have transferred control of the site to other people soon after he founded it. Ulbricht's lawyers contended that Dread Pirate Roberts was really Mark Karpelès, and that Karpelès set up Ulbricht as a fall guy. The presiding judge, Judge Katherine B. Forrest, did not permit any information that was speculative in nature from being entered into the case regarding whether Karpelès or anyone else ran Silk Road. With Judge Forrest's hardline stance, Ulbricht's attorneys faced an insurmountable legal challenge which was further exacerbated by FBI Agent Christopher Tarbell of the FBI's cyber-crime unit in New York calling Silk Road "the most sophisticated and extensive criminal marketplace on the Internet today." Mr. Ulbricht's fate appeared to be sealed as there was enormous pressure from all sides—the outcry of politicians, the judge's hardline stance, and investigative work done by FBI and former IRS agents, which doomed Ulbricht. Ultimately, Ulbricht was convicted on eight charges related to the Silk Road case. He was handed a draconian sentence of life in prison without the possibility of parole.

Legal authorities were casting a wide net to nab entrepreneurs of crypto currencies during that time, which may have been due to the negative attention brought on by the public and political outcry. Another champion for advancing virtual currency and the crypto industry was Charlie Shrem, Co-founder and CEO of Bitinstant. Charlie is also noted as being one of the original members of the Bitcoin foundation, a non-profit organization founded on the tenets to promote, standardize, and protect the use of Bitcoin cryptographic money for the advancement and benefit of users globally. Another member of this foundation that took a serious negative publicity hit with the hack of the Bitcoin exchange of Mt. Gox was CEO Mark Karpelès.

However, with such negative and sensationalized press, the market of crypto currencies experienced a flash crash with the price of Bitcoin falling to \$110.0. However, the price recovered peaking to \$200 only several weeks later. This trend showed that although illicit activity appeared to dominate the media coverage surrounding crypto currencies and Bitcoin, it was not the main driver. And with the FBI auctioning off 144,336 Bitcoins for a total value of around \$48 million, it legitimized Bitcoin as an actual alternative medium of exchange and an actual currency for Silicon Valley and venture capitalists.

The cases against the founders of crypto markets during the period between 2012 and 2015 with many receiving prison sentences serves as a warning to any entrepreneur brave enough to build a business around crypto currency to put a governance framework in place or face the possibility of prosecution. Who opens a business to go to jail?

As we investigate Silk Road and crypto currencies in general, it is clearly evident that Mr. Ulbricht discovered the secret sauce for widespread adoption of crypto currencies. Up until that time crypto currencies had more of a cult than mass appeal. The pathway for mass adoption had not been forged yet.

Building a Bitcoin environment similar to that of Satoshi Nakamoto or Hal Finney requires a considerable level of computer training and expertise. The probability of a mass population of common computer users, without any training on how to build a Bitcoin client, download the open-source software, build, compile, and successfully run the client without pulling out every strand of hair, is very low.

It is a masochistic process for the untrained computer user to use a command line for the purpose of transacting everyday business. Only a serious computer enthusiast and extremely principle-driven or ideal-driven cult-like groups would find pleasure in conducting daily transactions through a command line user experience.

Ross Ulbricht pioneered the way to onboard the masses by creating a portal that facilitated the widespread adoption of Bitcoin or crypto currencies as the medium of exchange. His innovation serves as a template for the industry to move forward, the ICO being the foundation for crypto operations.

ICOs are the current trend to make a digital currency offering available to the general public. The ICO or marketplace ring fences a targeted industry or business idea. The idea of creating a digital currency for no viable purpose other than trading is not very attractive. However, designing a marketplace that facilitates the use of goods and services through a crypto coin as the instrument that transfers value has become very attractive. The coin, having a perceived floor value within the given marketplace, provides an inherent store of value, and serves as the pathway for the adoption of a crypto coin as legitimate currency.

Creating ICOs appears to be the way forward for mass adoption. As we design the fundamental building blocks that make up an ICO, establishing the governance framework right from the origin would be wise. Attempting to backfill a governance framework is daunting and counterproductive. Let's briefly examine the composition of Silk Road that made it so effective. Silk Road utilized three interconnected networks for specific uses (Fig. 5.2).

Silk Road was the portal or network that provided a client experience and drove traffic to facilitate Bitcoin transactions.

It is important to note that the only entrepreneur who received prison sentences was the owner of the portal that facilitated deal making and not the exchange network or the payment network. It would be prudent to incorporate the governance framework before onboarding the first user into the network, even before the deal initiation point of the transactional work flow.

Fig. 5.2 Silk Road's three interconnected networks

To satisfy minimum requirements of KYC and AML, instituting a registration process for onboarding anyone coming into the network for any purpose is optimal. This registration process may appear to violate the privacy and anonymity ideals of digital network; however, providing a value-added business service is about compromise. It is in the best interest of anyone who takes the responsibility to register a domain that serves as the deal-making interface to a digital exchange or payment network to have a process in place that identifies individuals or entities operating within the network.

When dealing with any consumer personal information, cyber security has to be taken into consideration. As a safeguard, building the network upon a VPN (Virtual Private Network) is a wise choice. A VPN provides a safe passageway for a consumer device and internet server prohibiting eavesdropping during the data exchange even from the internet service provider. Offering this level of privacy protection for a consumer builds the confidence to use the network.

The benefits of preventing phishing and spying along with preventing data theft make building the portal on a VPN a logical choice. It is important to build these extra layers of protection when building these value-added services. It is also important to note that to utilize a crypto currency or to buy digital currencies an individual can open an account on an exchange and trade currencies using their digital wallet. Or download a build from Bitcoin.org and build a Bitcoin client and attempt a Bitcoin transaction. Most consumers will not interface through those mechanisms.

ICOs are value-added services and provide a pathway for stakeholders of the ICOs to implement a registration process for compliance. Trying to manage individuals or entities onboarded into the network at the individual level would be daunting as the network population grows. A more sustainable approach is to create a generalized set of groups to categorize the individuals onboarded into roles. These roles are important when presenting to compliance officers or any other legal official auditing the network. With role management it is possible to create a minimal set of rules engine toward instituting KYC and AML mechanisms.

To illustrate our marketplace and registration process, add a working context that allows certain critical features of building crypto marketplaces or

ICO building blocks. We will create a hypothetical pure dog breed coin. This coin will be called the lucky coin. In this marketplace or ICO the possible roles could be as follows:

- Portal Administrators—An organization registering the domain and administering the portal
- Initial Investors—The group from whom the initial seed funding to build the site and marketplace comes
- Dog Breeders—A breeder of pure dog breeds
- Canine Authentications service provider
- Caning Training service provider
- Dog buyer/owner

Roles as such create a comprehensive set of groups that any individual can be placed into while completing the onboarding process.

This publication is intended for a broad audience, to aid the non-technical reader building a working model, and as a backdrop to introduce these governance management concepts and facilitate understanding and act as guiding principles to design a marketplace with the minimal acceptable framework for regulators and government officials.

Participant Management

A social enterprise organization involves many participant individuals and bodies. Participant types are either delivery or receipt of benefits and services. Each participant has their own set of attributes and behaviors that includes information that is common across all the participant types and extra information that is applicable only to certain participant types.

Let's take an example of a dog center called "Lucky Dog Care" run by Mark. Lucky Dog Care has an end-to-end business model right from buying/adopting, training, breeding, grooming, walking, treatments, and so on. Mike has a white Dalmatian called Pepper. Pepper is a two-year-old and Mike wants him to learn certain behaviors. So, Mike engages Penny who works at Metro. Here we have four participants, namely, Mark, Mike, Pepper, and Penny. Each one of them carries a unique profile and is part of the Social Enterprise called Metro. They all share a common set of information such as Name, Age, Address, and so on, but in case of Pepper, there are certain extra attributes such as Breed, Size, and so on.

Mark wants to run his business on a digital currency. With the increased pressure to enforce machine learning and KYC laws, it is imperative that any entrepreneur thinking of creating a business based upon digital currencies build a governance framework to manage all participants utilizing the digital currency network or marketplace that drives user traffic to the client-facing portal. The severe and draconian-style sentences handed down in the Silk Road and other crypto cases prosecuted in 2014 is a testament and stern warning that law has a long and heavy arm that grinds as lawmakers around the globe work diligently to figure out a legal framework for crypto currencies and they will always rule heavily against money laundering and for KYC (Fig. 5.3).

Every participant should have a predetermined engagement in the organization through a proper intake process. Systems or domain platforms should be capable of governing the rights and protecting the values of the individuals. The fundamental building blocks of participant management at the minimum should comprise the following:

1. Role Management
2. Actions and Entitlements
3. Events and Activities

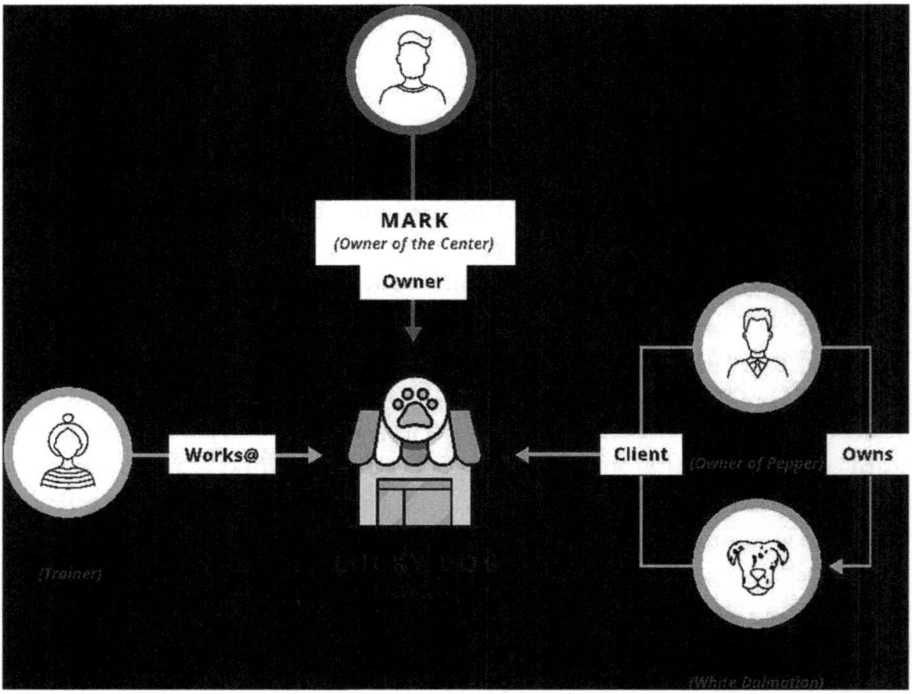

Fig. 5.3 Metro Dog Training Center

Role Management

Every participant in the system should be assigned a well-defined role. Role management helps with the management and authorization of all individuals utilizing the domain, which enables the specification and entitlement of resources that users in your application are allowed to access. Role management provides the platform the ability to manage individual users as groups and roles such as admin, customer, member, and so on. After the platform has established roles, the administrator can create access rules in your application. In our earlier example, Mark will set himself up as the owner or admin of the system, Mike will be a customer, Penny will be a staff and Pepper will be a member. Users can have multiple roles. For example, Mark can play the role of an owner as well as the admin of the system (Fig. 5.4).

The main purpose of establishing roles is to provide an easy way to manage access rules for groups of users. The portal provides the ability to create users and then administrators assign the users to roles. Now all the resources in the system can be restricted to permitted users only. Administrators can establish rules that grant and deny access to restricted resources. If someone tries to access a restricted resource, the user sees an error and his or her activity should be logged for audit purposes.

Now coming to the context of blockchain and more specifically crypto currencies, the role of management is extremely important. When we talk about roles in crypto currency, basically the utility tokens which are created to power your business transactions through an alternative mechanism of exchanging

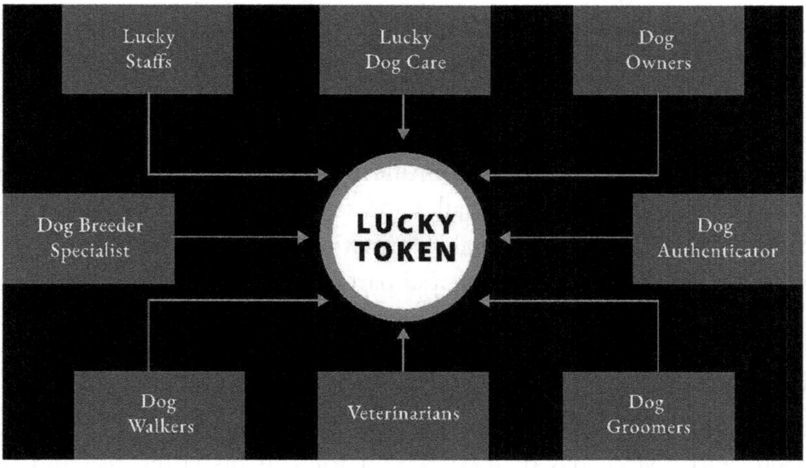

Fig. 5.4 Roles in the dog care marketplace

the values, it is highly necessary that your enterprise be aware of who has the possession of your tokens and how much is your circulating supply. In order to maintain granular transaction and holding information, the platform requires a comprehensive book of records. The platform can achieve that only by customizing a token that is governed by the foundational principles discussed in the previous section. One of these guiding principles is role management. The payment and accounting sides of crypto currencies are highly secure through consensus management and blockchain, but when it comes to the governance side of participants the picture is very weak. There is no specific regulation in place today that controls the flow of crypto currencies. In other words, values get transferred from one person to another through the electronic platform powered by miners and large computers worldwide but there is very little validation and traceability to display any sort of governance in the business activity. Many utility tokens that exist today are in a highly premature state based on the volume of trades that happen within their ecosystem. Most of it is driven by day traders over various crypto exchanges. In order to explain role management, let's take our Lucky Dog Center as an example.

Mark is setting up a new Utility token for his business called "LUCKY." Customers can buy the token from Mark at a certain price based on its usage. Before anyone can buy a token, Mark conducts a KYC process utilizing a registration workflow to identify and verify domain participants. This is the first and foremost step in role management where a person gets tagged to a role. According to the role he or she will gain different set of privileges in Mark's enterprise. The KYC process is the only way Mark can check the source of funds raised during the token sale by checking each buyer's identity and residency. This procedure is required not only by governments and regulators but also by the large corporations, banks, and public bodies we are bringing into the data trading market that is the Lucky Dog Center. To go through the registration process onboarding individuals will go through an information gathering portal that records basic identification such as personal information, address verification, electronic wallet address, and primary banking information. After capturing the minimal information for KYC, the next stage of the workflow is verification. The potential participant coming into the network is required to submit or upload documents that would be used as resources by the officials of the network to perform a background and verification check.

After onboarding is complete, users gain access to the system and are now ready to acquire LUCKY tokens. Let's say $1 can buy you 5 LUCKY tokens to begin with. Mark has defined certain roles in his enterprise and he has defined a set of principles around each role to implement the governance

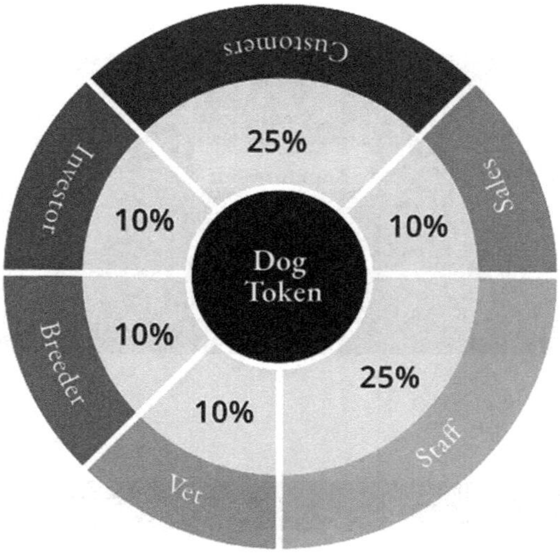

Fig. 5.5 DOG token circulation data

around his DOG token. The first principle that Mark wants to implement is to control the circulation of the DOG token across different stakeholders in the system. He can create new roles and route the token circulation as per his business demands. Figure 5.5 depicts a sample holding information of the DOG token. Another very important aspect of role-based participant management is that it will help to determine who was accessing the network, how they were accessing it, and where they were accessing it from, and then apply policies to control that level of access. For instance, applying a policy for access to staff members is different than what is granted for customer's access to your network. In our example Penny will have much more access to the system than Mike who is a customer. This entire process happens automatically in real time. It's invisible to the end user. There's no end-user intervention. They have no idea that this is even going on.

Actions and Entitlements

Once you define the roles, the next progressive step is to define actions that the role can perform. Actions are the business logics that comprise various decisions that result in a change of state for the entities involved. A simple example in our case would be Mike scheduling an appointment for Pepper. Mike is able to perform this action because he is in a role called "Client" (Fig. 5.6).

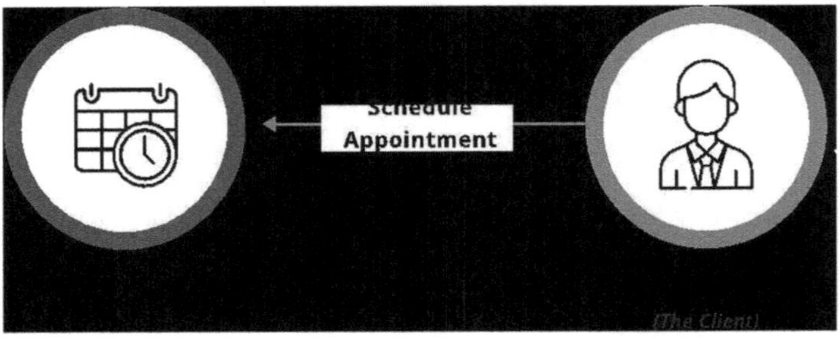

Fig. 5.6 Actions in role

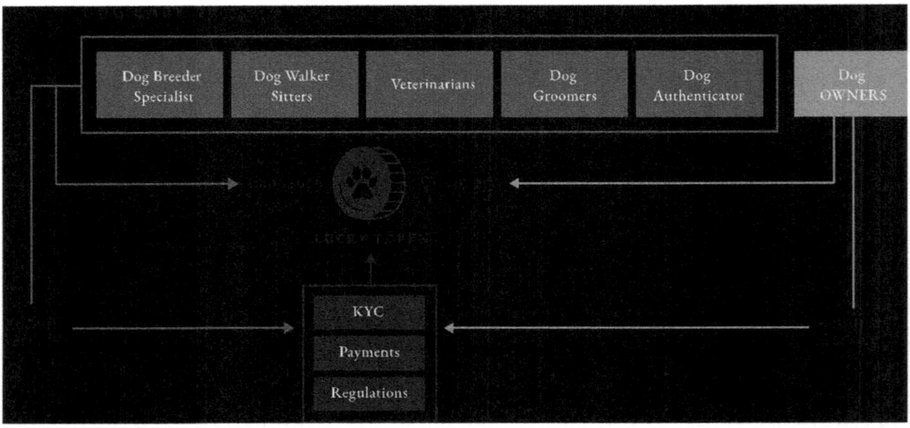

Fig. 5.7 Dog care business process

Similar to scheduling an appointment, there are several actions that are defined in the system and added to appropriate roles. Now this creates a basis for entitlements in the system ensuring that users with specific roles are entitled to perform respective actions. Let's now drill down into an action flow and determine how entitlement plays a major role in governing the business process (Fig. 5.7).

Both dog owners and service providers go through a proper KYC and role tagging and get listed in the LUCKY platform. Dog owners can search for the service providers and similarly service providers can search for appropriate job offers. Dog owners will need to acquire a certain number of LUCKY tokens before they can request for a service and they can buy tokens through the same platform at a market price based on demand and supply.

Let's now look at the actions and entitlement perspective of the LUCKY platform as a digital marketplace powered by blockchain. Every transaction that happens on the platform should have a specific value. So, the LUCKY platform has an entitlement model tied with actions (Fig. 5.8).

Customers with appropriate entitlements can perform permitted actions. Any user with FREE membership cannot engage in more than five services per month and should maintain a balance of at least ten LUCKY tokens. Premium members are the serious users of the platform with regular appointments for their dog with different service providers. Professional membership is for the other dog foundations and NGOs to engage with the platform with high volume of transaction capabilities. As their membership level increases, more information is captured during KYC and transactions are audited. This arrangement will ensure that there is a controlled traffic in the system and the enterprise can accordingly establish the required level of relationship with the customers to satisfy compliance and regulatory requirements (Fig. 5.9).

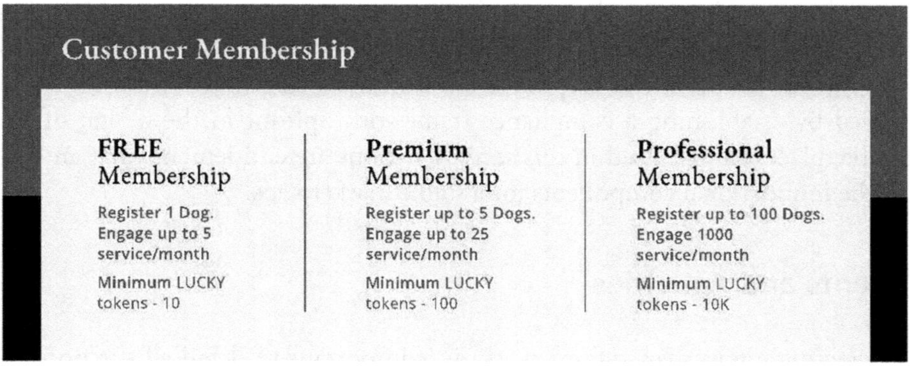

Fig. 5.8 Customer membership

Fig. 5.9 Service provider membership

Similar to customer membership, there exists service provider membership. According to entitlements a service provider will be able to engage himself or herself in the system. Again, free membership is for first-time users to try the system and does not require a lot of compliance whereas premium and professional memberships are the group of service providers that are serious about their business and want to grow their business using the LUCKY platform. Mark's enterprise can arrange for the necessary compliance and regulatory requirements as per the membership level.

The primary purpose of actions and entitlements in a digital currency paradigm is to implement the proper compliance and regulatory procedures. All the concepts discussed in this section apply to any enterprise trying to establish a digital currency in their business model. Legal authorities are casting a wide net for entrepreneurs of crypto currencies due to the negative attention brought in by the public and political outcry. Serving the public through an ICO or marketplace is the current major trend of the industry. Designing a marketplace that facilitates the use of goods and services through a crypto coin as the instrument that transfers value is invaluable. If the coin has a perceived floor value within the given marketplace that provides an inherent store of value, it serves the pathway for the adoption of a crypto coin as legitimate currency. Wisdom is better served by establishing a compliance framework upfront in the design of the marketplace. As discussed in this section, actions are entitlements that are one of the foundational components for a stable marketplace.

Events and Activities

In creating a governance framework, it is important to detail all the possible scenarios that are in the realm of the platform being generated. There are subtle differences between actions and events that must be pointed out. Actions are performed by users and only initiated by the user performing some action, such as place an order, or validate user, or transfer token to another user. Actions are assigned to roles. Events are platform- or system-generated outcomes that are a result of a user action and state the condition that defines certain tasks to be performed. For example, a user may attempt to place a buy order and the platform checks to see if there is enough account holding to place an order. The platform discovers there is not enough in the account so it throws a system-generated insufficient fund event. As a result of these events the system may perform a group of tasks.

A user can never invoke events directly. However, events are platform- or system-defined, and indirectly initiated as a result of a conditional response to

Fig. 5.10 Compliance requirements

a user action. Activities are the actual actions by participants. It is important to track an action every time it is performed by a participant in the activity list. The activity list is the tracking area of all the actions that have been undertaken by participants, Whether or not a user action is in compliance or violation is recorded by the platform. The purpose of tracking events and actions is to capture the platform state and generate a snapshot for any given point or period in time. Audit reports are integral for any compliance reporting platform. All the parts to perform compliance reporting should be in place. Reports can be created to generate participant types, list the daily activity details of participants by role, report on generated violations from events, and summarize participant activity for any period. The framework is comprehensive enough to identify any malicious activity or improper usage. Figure 5.10 illustrates five major compliance categories.

The five categories are indicative of requirements enforced by many regulatory bodies. Consumer protection is the main priority of security regulatory bodies to maintain market integrity and consumer confidence. These categories are required by federal and state laws, multiple asset trading rules, banking laws, and many other government agencies that require protection for the consumer and monetary systems. Money service businesses (MSBs) have come to the forefront of regulation. FinCEN (Financial Crimes Enforcement Network) has a fact sheet site that details the application of the Bank Secrecy Act (BSA) in regard to MSBs. Crypto exchanges can be seen as MSBs and are possibly subject to requirements of maintaining daily transaction reporting that is being defined by the Treasury and FinCEN. The regulatory guidelines being framed by these enforcement agencies could be perceived as a threat that undermines the privacy philosophy of the crypto currency community, one of the core tenets of crypto currency. Awareness of regulations targeting fraud protection (from hellion companies and organizations) and prevention of criminal activities involving terrorism and money laundering are always in focus. Thus it is optimal when operating any enterprise that can be categorized as an MSB to have a strong governance framework that lends well to reporting. Crypto currency will remain a hot topic where the major impetus is consumer protection and compliance. Regulators are tasked with creating a working balance between compliance and not impeding the rapid innovation of the technology.

Therefore, tracking actions, events, and activities is very important for any enterprise engaged in the business of digital currency.

The platform contains an ecosystem of technology that captures several pieces of critical information captured during every transaction. This data includes the IP address of the user, user agent, request header, user details, and transaction details. A categorization process occurs registering events as mission critical or as non-mission critical based upon request details. Logging occurs on every request as it is tracked and traverses through the workflow for processing. Combined information about events and activities serves as the vital information to construct the required compliance reports. Figure 5.11 depicts the compliance officer monitoring the customers, sellers, marketplace, blockchain, and other real-time transaction data that includes details such as what is being sold, who paid how much to whom, what are the IP address and geography of the parties, and so on.

The marketplace is designed upfront with a minimum level of governance. First it introduced the security of the environment through a properly secured network to face cybersecurity attacks with the protection of participant information. The data security measures are satisfied first with a VPN and HTTPS secured networks and by implementing best practices of encryption for transporting and storing data.

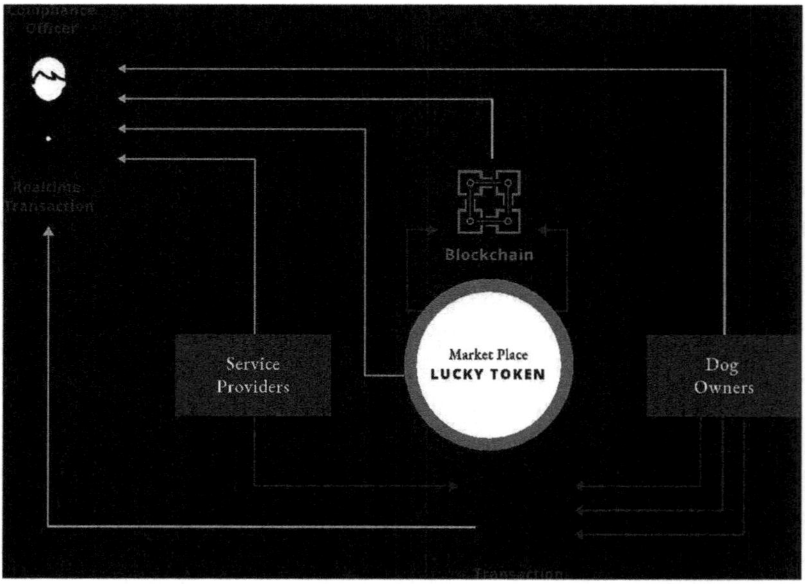

Fig. 5.11 Monitoring events and activities

The marketplace is providing a value-added service so compromise is needed with regard to anonymity with the owners of the network administrators. Having a role-based onboarding process to categorize individuals as users are onboarded into the network places profiles into proper categories based upon the participant types of the network or marketplace. This practice is very appealing to regulators as KYC is satisfied and participants are managed at the group level. Regulators and officials can assign restriction or limitations to groups, making the network much more governable. Architects of such digital currencies enterprises can create rules and engines at the group level, providing regulators a level of oversight for compliance.

The actions, events, and entitlements aid in creating the AML framework. Now that profiles are generated and categorized in the registration process, transactions that occur and may cause a certain breach event can be raised with actions taken based upon the specified event. The escalation process that captures profiles that may attempt to override certain limits based upon the profile or an attempt to perform a transaction that a profile is not entitled to will generate notifications within the network.

Having these safeguards inherently built into the network demonstrates to regulators and compliance officers a system of auditability. Entrepreneurs who take the approach of integrating an auditable system that meets regulatory requirements and best practices have the opportunity to help bring transparency to this marketplace.

6

Crypto Currency: The Birth of an ICO

Sarah Swammy, Richard Thompson, and Marvin Loh

Crypto Currency

By continuing the journey through defining, launching, and bringing a crypto currency to a level of critical mass, a symbiotic relationship between the currency and the marketplace is naturally developed. Crypto currencies exist only within the networks that they are conceived in. Those networks which give life to a particular currency will survive or have viability relative to the utility value of the marketplace. At least this will be apparent initially. Confusing the entire relationship as crypto currency is easy. However, deconstructing all the components is vital to bring clarity as an initial coin offering (ICO) is launched, and the number of crypto currencies increases in number. In Chap. 4, the importance of managing the marketplace through a well-defined governance mechanism was explored in depth. Chapter 5 defined what crypto currency is and what its types are. Since an ICO is the preferred choice to bring a crypto currency online, this chapter goes through the details of launching an ICO using the working model of LUCKY DOG coin for reference.

Electricity brought the concept of crypto currency to life officially when Liberty Standard assigned a value to Bitcoin based upon the cost of the electricity used to create this form of electronic money at $1309,03 (BTC) to 1 USD. A technological process called minting controls the creation and protection, as cryptology hides the identities of all its users. The digital coin, the item of value, is implemented on a blockchain: a specialized immutable, decentralized, anonymous, and trustless database. An enormous amount of computing capacity is required to execute a blockchain. Crypto currencies brought to light the power of blockchain technology and became the gas that powered the existence of blockchain networks.

S. Swammy et al., *Crypto Uncovered*, https://doi.org/10.1007/978-3-030-00135-3_6

The pet industry is an 86-billion-dollar market sector. A nice market to target for the launch of a digital currency. This coin will exist within the lucky.io network and serve as the instrument of value used to manage transactions. The coin will be a transactional token built on the Ethereum platform. Further explanations are forthcoming in later sections. A digital currency in this high-growth arena would prove beneficial to track retail activity, provide dog breed preferability information, track immunization, licensing, and registration details of dogs through the blockchain.

How Crypto Currency Works

Removing the cloud and hype around crypto currencies, and reducing it to its fundamental element, you discover it is an electronic accounting system containing entries that cannot be changed unless explicit criteria are fulfilled. Every transaction is broadcast immediately through the entire network. However, confirmation is achieved only through solving the hash function, which requires a finite amount of time to achieve. This consensus form of confirmation is a crucial concept native to crypto currencies.

This consensus type of transaction validation is the heart and soul of crypto currencies. Transactions go through a workflow of pending to be confirmed. A transaction can be modified while in pending. However, once transactions are confirmed, it is cemented into the blockchain. It is no longer forgeable. Neither can it be reversed, nor is it part of an immutable record of historical transactions: of the so-called blockchain.

Within the decentralized transaction network, miners are the only participants within the network to confirm transactions. Using Bitcoin as the reference from which all other crypto currencies are derived, miners are incentivized to perform transactions by being awarded at the current time 12.5 Bitcoin per confirmed transaction. This is their role within a crypto currency network. They take transactions, stamp them as legit, and spread them in the network. After a miner confirms a transaction, every node has to add it to its database. It has to become part of the blockchain. The underlying data structure is an encrypted hash database called a Merkle Tree. In theory, anyone can be a miner. A decentralized network does not have any authority to delegate this task. Hence a crypto currency needs some mechanism to prevent one ruling party from abusing it. If there were no controls in place to prevent the spread of forged and fraudulent transactions from spreading, the system would break immediately.

Crypto currencies are entries about tokens in decentralized consensus databases. They are called CRYPTO currencies because strong cryptography secures the process. Cryptography is used to develop crypto currencies. They

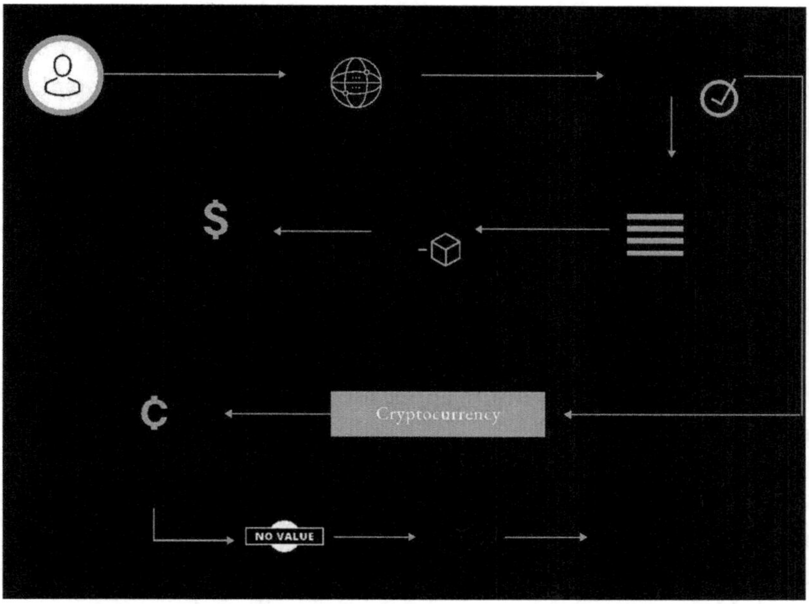

Fig. 6.1 How crypto currency works

are secured by math. Because of the security, it is near to impossible that a Bitcoin address will be compromised.

Figure 6.1 depicts a very high-level overview of crypto currency.

Types of Crypto Currency

Each crypto currency solves a particular problem and fits into one of the following three categories:

1. Transactional
2. Platform
3. Utility tokens

Some crypto currencies can be fit into more than one category. The categories along with some examples are discussed below.

Transactional

It is known as the original category for crypto currencies. These are mainly designed to be used as money and thus exchanged for goods and services. Some transactional crypto currencies are Bitcoin, Litecoin, and a host of others.

This category of crypto currencies is intended to eliminate the need for government-issued currency. It is quite a possibility that some form of crypto currency may replace some or all fiat currencies one day. But the replacement cryptos may still come from central banks—Singapore's government, for one, is testing out this idea with its Project Ubin.

Platform

Platform crypto currencies are designed to eliminate intermediaries. Markets are also created using these and even used for launching other crypto currencies. The base for a host of future applications is provided by platform crypto currencies.

One of the prime examples of a platform crypto currency is Ethereum. A decentralized platform like Ethereum is used for running smart contracts. A smart contract is a kind of application that runs precisely as programmed. Hence the possibility of fraud, censorship, or even downtime is significantly reduced. Many new crypto currencies are also built on Ethereum.

Utility Tokens

A particular task is performed by utility crypto currency. An example of a utility crypto currency is Ripple (XRP). It is designed to facilitate fiat money transfer in an economical and highly efficient manner. Multiple banks and institutions also use it. Some of the names include UBS, Santander, BMO, and American Express. Tech investor Nick Tomaino believes utility tokens can be broken down into four different categories:

- **Asset tokens**
  Traditional asset tokens are the crypto representations of standard fiat assets.
- **Usage tokens**
  Usage tokens provide digital service access. Bitcoin is considered a usage token because users are granted access to a virtual payments network.
- **Work tokens**
  Work tokens offer users the right to contribute work to a decentralized organization. For example, Maker, a work token, serves as the backstop in a collateralized debt system.
- **Hybrid tokens**
  Hybrid tokens are a mix of usage and work coins. They can be used for multiple purposes.

Ethereum

Similar to Bitcoin, Ethereum is a distributed public blockchain network. Some significant technical differences exist between the two, but the most important distinction to note is that Bitcoin and Ethereum differ substantially in purpose and capability. Bitcoin offers one particular application of blockchain technology, a peer-to-peer electronic cash system that enables online Bitcoin payments. While the Bitcoin blockchain is used to track ownership of digital currency (Bitcoins), the Ethereum blockchain focuses on running the programming code of any decentralized application. In the Ethereum blockchain, instead of mining for Bitcoin, miners work to earn Ethereum, a type of crypto token that fuels the network. Beyond a tradable crypto currency, Ethereum is also used by application developers to pay for transaction fees and services on the Ethereum network.

The Ethereum Virtual Machine, which is Ethereum's core innovation, is a Turing complete software that runs on the Ethereum network. You can run any program, regardless of the programming language, given enough time and memory. The Ethereum Virtual Machine makes the process of creating blockchain applications much more accessible, and it is also more beneficial than ever before. Ethereum enables the development of potentially thousands of different applications all on one platform, and so you don't have to build an entirely original blockchain for each new application. It gives allowance to the developers to build and deploy decentralized applications. A decentralized application or DAPP serves some particular purpose for its users. Bitcoin, for example, is a DAPP that provides its users with a peer-to-peer electronic cash system. Online Bitcoin payments are also possible through it. The code of decentralized applications runs on a blockchain network. This means that they are not controlled by any individual or central entity.

Ethereum can decentralize any services that are centralized. Many intermediary services that exist across hundreds of different industries include apparent bank services like loans. This also includes intermediary services like title registries, voting systems, regulatory compliance, and much more. Decentralized Autonomous Organizations (DAOs) can also be made using Ethereum. A DAO is fully autonomous, with no single leader. They are run by programming code, on a collection of smart contracts. These smart contracts are written on the Ethereum blockchain. The code is designed to replace the rules and structure of a traditional organization, eliminating the need for people and centralized control. Everyone who purchases tokens owns a DAO, but instead of each token equating to equity shares and ownership, tokens act as contributions that give people voting rights.

Decentralized applications running on the Ethereum blockchain benefit from all of its properties.

- **Immutability**—A third party cannot make any changes to data.
- **Corruption and tamper proof**—Apps are based on a network formed around the principle of consensus, which in turn makes it impossible to censor.
- **Secure**—With no central point of failure and secured using cryptography, applications are well protected against hacking attacks and fraudulent activities.
- **Zero downtime**—Apps never go down and can never be switched off.

Though decentralized applications bring a lot of benefits, they aren't faultless. Humans write smart contract code. So they are only as good as the people who write them. Unintended adverse actions can be taken because of code bugs or oversights. There is no way in which an attack or exploitation can be stopped if a mistake in the code gets exploited. It can be stopped either by obtaining a network consensus or by rewriting the underlying code. It goes against the essence of the blockchain which is meant to be immutable. Also, any action taken by a central party raises serious questions about the decentralized nature of an application.

Smart Contract

In the founding days of blockchain, Nick Szabo envisioned that smart contracts would be integral components of the technology. Blockchain is the core payment system and decentralized record-keeping technology of crypto currencies. However, it does not address the standardization of data content as more complex transactions enter the blockchain. Anyone can imagine as crypto currencies are utilized as payments for unstructured products, such as a bond with an embedded call option, that the description of the transaction must become more sophisticated as the type of transaction. These digital contracts, also referred to as self-executive contracts, would contain not only the physical economic terms between two parties but also settlement instructions, penalties, and rules that govern the enforcement of the transaction. The founders conceptualized a need for a computer program to control the transfer of the nominal units between two parties. That premise became the basis

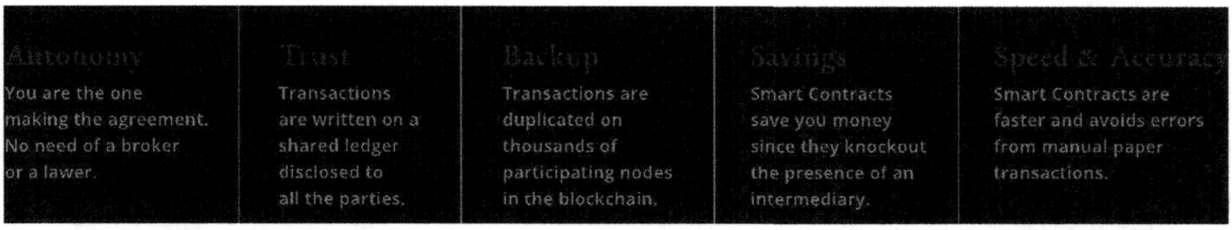

Fig. 6.2 Benefits of a smart contract

of smart contracts. Computer code is embedded within the details of the contract and distributed throughout the network that computes and manages the blockchain.

At a DC blockchain summit in 2016, the Ethereum smart contract was detailed by its founder, Vitalik Buterin, outlining the workflow of how an asset or currency is transferred into a program. At some point in time, the program runs and automatically validates a condition as to how the asset is awarded, testing if the asset should go to one party or a third party set within the rules of the contract or if it should be immediately refunded to the original party. As in the case of our working model Lucky coin, a contract may have conditions pending passing a physical examination by a determined veterinarian. Coins are transferred from Escrow to a designated breeder. If there is a physical failure by pure breed dog, tokens are returned to the original party. The blockchain records and replicates the document which gives it specific security and immutability. Figure 6.2 illustrates the importance of a smart contract.

Popular implementation of a smart contract is the ESCROW account. Let's take the case of an employer and consultant situation. Consultant wants to be sure that the employer pays him by the end of the month and the employer is not sure about the consultant's talent to deliver the service. Employer moves the money to the ESCROW account that ensures the consultant that the employer has enough funds to pay him when he delivers the work and the employer is not worried because if the consultant does not deliver the promised work, then the funds go back to the employer's account (Fig. 6.3).

New crypto currency venture funds are raised by using this. An ICO is used by startups to bypass the rigorous and regulated capital-raising process required by venture capitalists or banks. A percentage of the crypto currency is sold to early backers of the project in exchange for legal tender or other crypto currencies, but usually for Bitcoin or Ethereum. This can also be stated as initial public coin offering (IPCO).

An ICO is used for crowdfunding a new crypto currency and an innovative idea perfect for implementing on the blockchain technology (mostly, as of

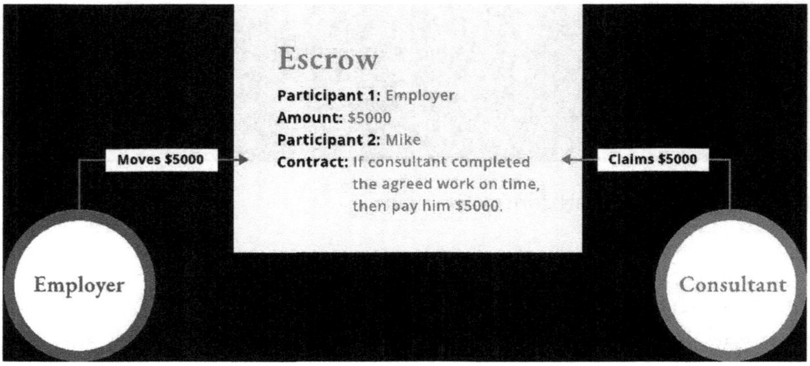

Fig. 6.3 Smart contract versus ESCROW

now). If you are familiar with IPOs (initial public offerings) in the traditional stock market, you'll understand that an ICO is a little similar, yet different, concept but for crypto currencies. When some genius developers and entrepreneurs come into contact with each other and generate a brilliant idea, tokens for a new crypto currency are offered by them so that they can gather enough funding to convert their idea into reality. The significant difference between ICOs and IPOs is that when you invest you get tokens of that new crypto currency which may get listed on the exchanges once the idea has been developed. It means they aren't granting you any ownership in the company like IPOs do.

The event of an ICO usually runs for one week or more. Here everyone is allowed to purchase tokens by exchanging established crypto currencies like Bitcoin (BTC) or Ethereum (ETH) just like in the case of IPOs of the traditional stock market. A specific goal or limit can be present for project funding, which means that every token will have a predesignated price that will not change during the ICO period, which also means that the token supply is static. Usually, the number of tokens to be distributed are denoted by the company. For example, 40–50% of the tokens are allocated in the ICOs; 10–20% go to the development team and their efforts to make the project work; 20–30% stay reserved for future use purposes. Let's look at some of the popular and successful ICOs in the past.

1. **The Ethereum ICO** in 2014 delivered the first ICO that introduced the smart contract officially and raised 18 million Bitcoins that were valued at $0.40 per Ethereum. It was one of the first of its kind to put this concept of an ICO on the map. In 2014, the Ethereum project was announced. Its ICO

raised $18 million in Bitcoin at $0.40 per Ethereum. The project went live in the year 2015, and 2016 witnessed Ethereum's value going up to $14 with a market capitalization of over $1 billion. Ever since receiving that amount of funding, Ethereum has quickly grown successfully to become the second-most valuable crypto currency ecosystem in the world today.

2. **Golem Project.** Raising $8.6 million in mere minutes is quite a fantastic thing. Golem project will be remembered for achieving that objective. Given that Golem is a decentralized global market for computing power, this significant amount of interest was not entirely unexpected. The ICO was launched at $0.01 and raised $8,596,000, selling 820,000,000 tokens within a few minutes. Presently, the token is valued at $0.512 stating the ROI of +5019.10%.
3. **LISK,** the world's first modular blockchain-based platform allows developers to create their apps and run them on sidechains (this is a good thing). Programmers choose its apps as they are built with Javascript. Many of the key players from Ethereum were on board, and, consequently, the ICO went down a treat. After successfully raising $5.8 million in four weeks at the price of $0.076 per token, Lisk's ROI currently sits at 19,080%.

How to Launch an ICO

ICOs are also thought of as a tool for any project by some startup owners. Money can be quickly raised and the lengthy and expensive process of registering an IPO with the regulatory agencies bypassed. It used to be the case during the formative days of the ICO market, but now it's no longer true. ICO is not a tool that can be quickly raised. The ICO ethos is taking shape, and industries are adopting informal standards. The central question every startup considering an ICO should ask itself is whether they can integrate digital tokens into their business model in a meaningful way. If the only use for your coin is to trade on an exchange, it guarantees that the price will crash soon after the ICO takes place. As soon as any token released during a campaign hits the market, it will come under tremendous speculation. Strong demand for the token, is the one thing that can defend a demand that can be produced by the real utility. Authenticity and transparency are among the many core pillars of the crypto currency community. And that also includes the ICO market. Due to this, an ICO whose only objective is to enrich the project owners at the expense of the contributors will not receive any positive attention.

Following are the seven significant steps for launching an ICO.

1. Build the Product
2. Write the White Paper
3. Perform Legal Checks
4. Create the Token
5. Security Audit
6. Leadership
7. Manage the Community

Build the Product

Hustlers who are trying to raise capital as quickly as possible tend to ignore this crucial step. The most crucial part of an ICO is building an actual product. You should spend your time making a stable, robust, secure, and scalable product on the blockchain. Then only can you tell us how it's going to change the world. Perhaps you can get away with launching an MVP or beta and then conduct your token sale. But I think it's safe to say that a little equity investment has to be raised by most startups to start off their business. When we want to make money, we also require money. And this is no exception. You must have a product, and your token must be used by your product. Let's take our use case from the last chapter of the LUCKY coin and build the product abstract.

The LUCKY coin is an Ethereum-based blockchain platform regulated by smart contracts. The platform supports the Dog community by building and creating solutions devoted to improving the quality of Dog care worldwide. The blockchain gives LUCKY coin the power to change the world for the better. LUCKY coin develops the Dog world as well as creates market intelligence through a crypto currency reward system that inspires participation throughout the community. The LUCKY coin is the first crypto currency that uses a decentralized review platform and transparently rewards owners and veterinarians who make contributions that benefit the community. The LUCKY coin Foundation team firmly believes in building a future health care world that will fall into the hands of the people. This will result in the disruption of the existing industries and the creation of new industries in the short and long term. LUCKY coin expects the platform to improve Dog health and hygiene habits drastically, thus improving the quality of life for individuals resulting in improved overall health and increased longevity.

Write the White Paper

A white paper can be described as a guidebook that clearly outlines the technical aspects of the product. It also includes the problems it intends to solve, how it is going to address them, a description of the team, and a story of the token generation and distribution strategy. To summarize, we can say that it is a pitch deck, a business plan, a marketing plan, and a technical manual all at once. So there might be a question in your mind as to why so many terrible white papers are being published. From personal experience, I can tell you that writing a white paper is NOT easy. These are seriously complex documents, and far too few teams are investing into proper writers and marketers. Hiring vetted external writers can force the founders to be more rigorous and thorough, while bad vendors will cover up gaps in thinking or product inefficiencies with jargon and fluff. If a white paper were to be written for LUCKY coin to set the stage for the world's first pet coin, the white paper should thoroughly explain a new conceptual framework to be used within the Dog world for organizational purposes. It should start something like below:

> Through the utilization of recent technological innovations, we have created a model with the ability to overcome the majority of the Dog industries' major constraints and, furthermore, propose various measures that will significantly improve the efficiency of Dog practice, thus improving the owner's level of Pet well-being. LUCKY coin strives to create a Dog world community by rewarding people who provide valuable contributions with crypto currency. By using this reward system, the foundation will see a rise in a currency which in turn will reach a broad market, including a vast number of people who have yet to participate in any crypto currency economy.

According to *Harvard Business Review*, "To protect the blockchain vision from political pressure and regulatory interference, blockchain networks rely on a decentralized infrastructure that can't be controlled by any one person or group."

> The integration of Dog owners and the associated marketplace of service providers is an astounding concept. It requires the creation of a community in which transparency and shared responsibility can take place. The Metro Dog Foundation's core missions are to improve the quality of Dog care worldwide, reduce pet care and treatment costs, and create a Dog community. The LUCKY Token will be created to help assist the Metro Dog Foundation with

the missions mentioned above by giving power to the people. LUCKY coin focuses on developing some tools, each one targeting a different sector of the Dog world. These tools are used by individuals who will receive LUCKY Tokens as a reward. They can later use to pay for their Pet treatment or to purchase Pet products. The primary objective is not to compete with other crypto currencies, but rather to provide a solution and support for the Dog care services worldwide through a blockchain. The Metro Dog Foundation is interested in evaluating the actual substance and value that can be created with a coin (LUCKY) that represents the health of all individuals. The LUCKY coin will be both a FinTech and a logistic platform of the global Dog world. The Foundation's exact contribution in ERC20 coins (LUCKY) used for Dog projects will be provided later on in the white paper.

Customer feedback is an essential part of all service industries aiming at long-term success. The Pet care World is no exception. No regulatory authority, no central institution, no powerful organization or individual can control the world better than the owner community. Trust among people is more valuable to the world players than constant, trustworthy feedback from the owners. A community is required for this to be achieved and this is where LUCKY coin steps in. LUCKY coin emphasizes the world's challenges and reveals the solutions for increasing Pet practice's efficiency. Implementing a blockchain-based industrial crypto currency can incentivize the world in solving the majority of the existing and future constraints. The four phases of implementation each with its milestones, goals, and focus are mentioned below.

We will stop here with the white paper sample. That's how a white paper is prepared, highlighting the platform features and benefits followed by the project milestones. Mentioned below is a sample roadmap for the LUCKY coin launch. Roadmap is a must-have in any white paper (Fig. 6.4).

That said, neither the white paper nor any other business collateral holds more weight than a working proof of concept. So, don't stop with the white paper; develop a working prototype and demonstrate the concept that will drive more people to participate in your ICO.

Fig. 6.4 LUCKY coin roadmap

Perform Legal Checks

The well-known phrase "leave it up to the professionals" is often said and sometimes heeded. However, when it comes to registering and creating ICOs and digital currencies this is advice to adhere to strictly. The Securities and Exchange Commission (SEC) does not officially recognize ICOs. Any interpretation that a communication is conveyed related to a security being offered, or any funder who may actually fund an ICO construes the message that an asset that yields a return other than what is being proposed is the funding of a token with no value and can be legally fatal to the issuer of the ICO. Entrepreneurs beware; let the legal professional, such as Cooley, Perkins Coie, and K&l Gates, all of whom have built strong reputations in navigating the legal minefield of ICO registration, perform this necessary function. No entrepreneur, looking to launch an ICO, wants any perception to be created through inadvertent communication that many have any funder thinking that they are buying an asset. Only a token that facilitates market transactions within the market network is being funded. No communications about a possible increase in prices or demonstrations of returns can ever be made. The legal professionals will draft the legal description and the token and construct the message to what the funders are receiving. Allowing the professionals to facilitate process and remaining transparent with all funders helps to avoid trouble from the regulators, such as the SEC of FinCEN. The governance framework established to manage participants to satisfy KYC and AML requirements and continuance of good compliance policy needs to be maintained during registration. SAFT (Simple Agreement for Future Tokens) has become an industry framework, designed and created by the legal stalwart Cooley; in particular, it has become an instrument and open-source legal framework for token sales. There are no global standards for ICOs and the registration and launching process varies from country to country. Put the effort in to comply with all relevant laws and regulations to remain clear of any legal ramifications. Following the best practices as a guideline is wise. Wiki your counsel and team:

- Investigate to determine if the token you are offering during the ICO appears as security or not? What actions are necessary to alleviate the concerns that the token may be secure?
- Target specific audiences during the token sale (geo-fencing).
- It is a good practice to establish a foundation to champion the token.

Soliciting unregistered securities in the US can result in hefty fines and severe prison sentences. Nothing to be taken lightly or for granted. In the US, securities are heavily regulated and selling unregistered securities can result in significant fines and prison sentences. If a company develops a token and the company can distribute tokens at the time of the ICO, then the token is probably not secure, and there is not much problem. The company can crowdfund via an ICO just like Golem and accept money from anyone. However, if a company is raising funds to develop the token with a promise to distribute tokens to investors in the future, then it is conducting a token presale and not an ICO. The problem is that if a company is doing a token presale, it will possibly be seen as selling securities under the US Howey Test[1] and will run into various SEC securities restrictions and potentially costly security registration and/or reporting requirements. To not be subject to US law, which may be applicable to foreign companies if they are seen as a Foreign Private Issuer by the SEC, some companies have incorporated outside the US and excluded US investors from their token presale. DFINITY, a Swiss organization, took this approach in their token presale stating "Due to regulatory uncertainty, you must not be a US person by citizenship or residency."

Alternatively, a company can choose to be subject to, and comply with, US securities law to legally accept money from US investors in a token presale. **CoinList** (a platform for token-backed networks to raise funds through pre-launch token sales) and the **SAFT** aim to streamline US securities regulatory compliance and make it easy for companies to accept money from US investors in token presales legally. SAFT is modeled after the YC Simple Agreement for Future Equity (SAFE), which has become a standard angel and seed round investment agreement used by startups. SAFE promises investors future equity, while SAFT will seemingly promise investors future tokens.

Create the Token

Creating the token is the most straightforward part of the ICO process. When a token is created at its core, it means you have created an asset that your business needs to survive. Tokens can represent any tradable good. This includes digital coins, loyalty points, gold certificates, IOUs, in-game items, and so on. Tokens are somewhat similar to shares of a company sold to investors in an IPO transaction.

You should decide on certain things before creating anything. This includes how much you want to raise, the number of blockchain or Ethereum tokens

[1] The Howey Test is a test created by the Supreme Court for determining whether certain transactions qualify as investment contracts and their applicable registration and disclosure requirements under the Securities Act of 1933 and Securities Exchange Act of 1934.

you will issue, the number of tokens you are planning to retain for the team. The number of tokens you are planning to sell within the pre-ICO (if you decide to sell some of the tokens before the main ICO). It should also be agreed in advance in what scenario you will issue additional tokens. There are several platforms, such as Ethereum and waves, that allow you to create your tokens without having to create a blockchain from scratch. Smart contract controls the sale of these tokens. It is a computer program which can directly control the transfer of digital assets between parties under certain conditions.

Creating the initial value for the token is a very complicated process. We should consider a lot of options. It is called the tokenization process. Tokenization includes defining a unit of value to represent a specific asset. Within the blockchain and crypto currency space, tokens act as a computing protocol in which developers can digitally assign a token to become a medium for value exchange within a network of users. The critical differentiator for any tokenization effort is designing a crypto-economic reason for the token to exist and have real utility, beyond its speculative trading value. Crypto-economics is about aligning incentives of using a token system to encourage beneficial behaviors among all participants.

Though tokenization has recently become a buzzword, it can't be considered as a new concept. As recently as 1950, the US was home to thousands of functioning forms of tokenized currency. Individual banks would issue banknotes; industrial and agricultural trading companies would issue "scrip" to help streamline transactions; and government, retail, and property brokers would offer alternate forms of currency to replace illiquid government-issued currency. For instance, the US dollar, after moving off a gold-backed standard, became a long-standing example of a traditional asset token. A dollar tokenized on the blockchain should have a value of about a dollar. But given the instantaneous rate of exchange possible in a distributed network of servers, like blockchain, even minor fluctuations in price over time can create arbitrage opportunities between the value of a token and the asset it represents.

Due to the ICOs and token generation events (TGEs), tokenization has become a hot topic. In these events, a new crypto currency, digital coin, or token that investors can purchase as an investment in the company will be issued by a company. Hence, the company can raise millions of dollars in capital without using the conventional VC funding model. The rapid growth of crypto currency is attracting investors and founders. They want to be a part of the next big thing. Many government regulatory agencies around the world have also been attracted. More clarity is still required in how tokens should be designed and represented to potential buyers. If the industry for companies and investors focuses on the value of the token within its network, it will be more useful to them. Some tokens that are intrinsically designed to support

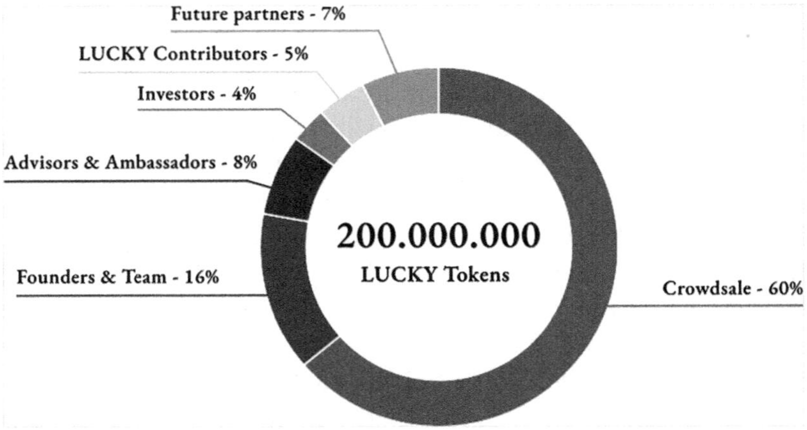

Fig. 6.5 Sample token economics

the specific business purpose of the project has more potential to be on the right track for long-term growth.

Let's do the token economics for LUCKY coin. LUCKY team will generate by Ethereum smart contract an ERC20 standard token LUCKY Coin (LUCKY). All wallets supporting Ethereum, including Jaxx, MyEtherWallet.com, and Ethereum Wallet, support ERC20 compliant tokens. The ICO contract will be directly linked to the token contract so that instant issuance of tokens will be possible. Users will be able to see in real time how many tokens they will get in return to their contribution and will not need to wait for an extended period to get them (sending will be enabled immediately after the ICO ends) (Fig. 6.5).

- Total number of generated LUCKY will be 200,000,000
- 60% of tokens will be sold in the ICO to secure funds for further product development, operations, and international expansion
- 16% of tokens will be held by the project founders and the rest of the team that helped to develop the project with their hard work and dedication
- 4% of tokens will be given to early stage angel investors, true believers, who showed a lot of trust and provided rocket fuel for our idea
- 5% of tokens is intended for the initial stocking of the bounty pool to award contributors, who help build and curate our database of entities
- 8% of tokens will be awarded to our advisors and ambassadors that helped the project with their knowledge and expertise
- 7% of tokens will be reserved for future partners who will join the project at a later stage All tokens belonging to founders, employees, and seed investors will be reversely vested for 24 months with monthly cliffs

The tokens that remain unsold will be transferred into the marketing budget. Tokens will be locked into a smart contract and accessible after one year when the global marketing campaign will begin. The lockdown is to prove to the contributors that we believe in the value of the vibe and as reassurance that the tokens won't be sold immediately and will be spent only for marketing and sales activities.

Security Audit

An audit measures whether your organization is following good data protection practice. An audit helps organizations to identify whether they have effective policies and procedures in place. The code is reviewed by experts to ascertain if the code is secure where they check the possibility of any existing vulnerabilities, future bugs, or any errors in coding that could expose users.

Due to the complexity of a new programming environment, it is possible for even expert developers to make mistakes when writing code. It becomes critical to verify correctness using unit testing and tooling validation.

Some of the leading smart contract security auditing companies are mentioned below. Each one of them is known for their strengths. As a business owner, you will need to research before hiring the advisory company to help you achieve your goals.

1. New Alchemy is known as a strategy and technology advisory company that specializes in tokenization.
2. Solidified.io is a crowdsourcing company where any developer can submit their code for comprehensive quality review by a community of qualified and certified experts.
3. Coinfabrik is a firm that helps other firms to develop smart contracts. It is also involved in the development of hyper ledger, the private blockchain, supply chain blockchain, wallet protection, loan data sharing, and safe, reliable crypto exchanges in addition to helping with smart contract audits.
4. Zeppelin reviews code and develops a report on the quality of a company's code, and the result is published online—same is the case with New Alchemy.
5. Token Market provides a complete token launching set of services including creating tokens, developing and auditing smarty contracts, and hosting crowd sale, among other services.

Leadership

The team is the essential part of any project. After taking a look at what the project aims to solve along with the crowd sale structure and token utility, it's always important to make sure a programmer is present in the team or at least knows the technical requirements of a blockchain project.

Blocklancer's CEO/Co-founder makes it very easy to understand whether or not the project has team members who can navigate the space. He's a computer scientist and also a university graduate on the topic. The project also has other technically versed members, but a Technical Founder is someone, in my experience, venture capitalists and angel investors want to have in a tech startup they're deciding to invest in.

Blocklancer's Founder made sure to put his face out there from the beginning. He also did an interview with CryptoCandor in which he explained essential facets of the Blocklancer ecosystem in detail. This is like the all-time best confirmation any ICO investor can see in a project because it ensures that their CEO/Lead Developer exists!

Manage the Community

It is probably the second-most important step in the ICO process. Token sales depend on the investors, and hence it is essential to note that to make your token sales to reach somewhere, enough investors should know about it. It is sad, but a fact, that initial hype drives the majority of token sales. This hype ideally should be supported by investors that support both you and your token, and will not sell at the first opportunity. The ICO marketing channels that I would suggest investing time and resources into are as follows:

Forums The most famous is Bitcointalk, where practically all the ICO projects are run. You will receive many reviews—positive and negative—but they will help you to improve your project.

ICO Calendars Lists of "top ICOs" are often created by bloggers and journalists (https://itsblockchain.com/top-5-upcoming-icos-to-invest-in/) by the data from specific ICO calendar sites mentioned below:

Coinschedule.com	CoinGecko.com	Cyber Fund	ICOCrowd.com
ICOCountdown.com	ICO-List.com	Coinlist.com	

Quora Discussions A platform like Quora can play an important role here. Many discussions exist on Quora about different ICOs and specific crypto currencies. You can actively participate in these discussions and link back to your ICO landing page.

Slack and Telegram Your channel on Slack and Telegram must be created in your communications strategy. Potential investors live on these channels and will be able to connect with the project's founders, team members, and also with one another. Monitoring these channels at all times is crucial. All questions and false accusations raised by users must be answered promptly.

Media Coverage Good PR can help a company in various ways. Quality PR in the right media outlets is required to help establish credibility and to position your company as an innovator and thought leader. It also has the potential to convince people of your business model. The mainstream media are becoming more and more cynical about ICOs. Thus having a great story outside of the ICO is critical. It is crucial to make sure to communicate with your audience both before and throughout the campaign. Also, be mindful that pre-ICO media is quite different than the post-ICO press, as the target demographic changes.

ICO Crowd Sale

A successful crowd sale is judged by the pre-allotment of tokens reserved by the ICO transferring from the assigned account of the ICO to the accounts of all investors participating in the ICO that accurately reflects the purchase amount and the funds from the investor transferring to the funding account of the ICO. Immediately after the ICO crowd sale event, a reconciliation process happens to ensure delivery of tokens and transfer of funds. If there are no errors or exceptions and initial investors are satisfied with receiving their assigned tokens, a successful ICO crowd sale has occurred.

Ethereum Development Model

Traditionally application development is being laid with a centralized server for managing and serving all the requests. A hosting provider is required to host your web application for which there are hosting providers like AWS, Heroku, or a VPS. All the clients interact with this one central application.

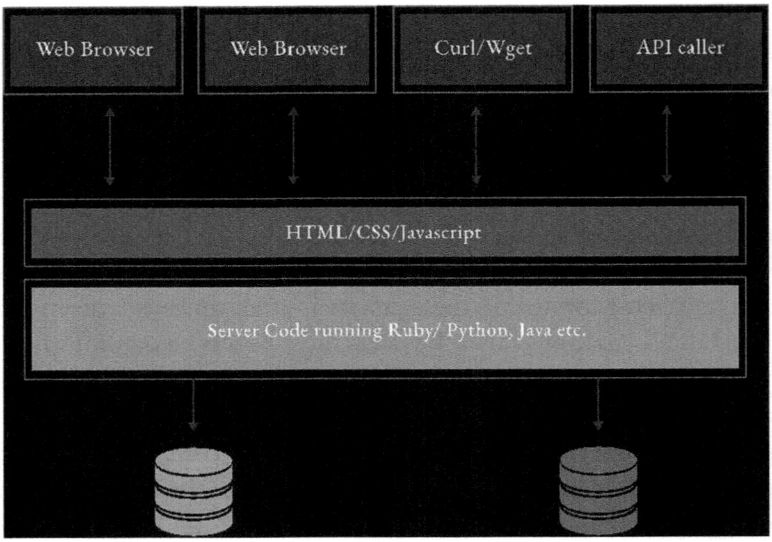

Fig. 6.6 Traditional centralized application development

Clients can be a browser or another API consuming your service. When a client requests the server, the server does its magic, talks to the database and/or cache, reads/writes/updates the database, and serves the client.

Most of the times this architecture works very well. However, there are specific applications where it would be beneficial if that database was publicly and securely accessible by everyone and you don't have to rely on this web app owner for your data (Fig. 6.6).

Let's take eBay as an example. Consider yourself a power seller who has earned hundreds of good reviews. But for some reason, your account got suspended by eBay. That would be very bad and could severely impact your business. In this situation it would be nice if all your reviews and ratings could be moved to another platform (say eBay Competitor). Though eBay is a popular and trusted third party between buyers and sellers, each sale includes a commission for them. Imagine if there was a way to eliminate eBay from the transaction between buyer and seller. This way, you can save the amount you are spending on commission. Your data can also be accessed. Here decentralized applications (DAPPS) come into the picture. DAPPS (decentralized applications) can be built very easily using Ethereum. If you notice, every client (browser) tends to communicate with its instance of the application. No central server is present for all clients to connect to. This means a full copy of the blockchain running on their computer/phone and so on will be needed by

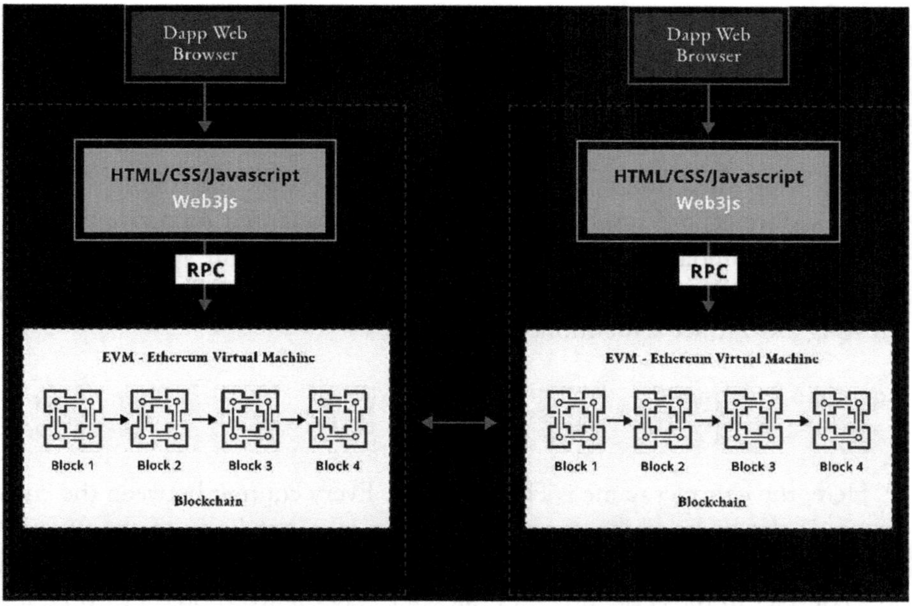

Fig. 6.7 Ethereum development model

every person who wants to interact with a DAPP. That means before an application can be used, the entire blockchain has to be downloaded, and then you can start using the application. Initially this might sound ridiculous, but it has the advantage of not relying on a single central server. Figure 6.7 highlights a reference model of an Ethereum DAPP at a high level.

Solidity Programming Language

Solidity is a high-level language whose syntax is similar to that of JavaScript, and it is designed to compile the code for the Ethereum Virtual Machine. Solidity is a statically typed, contract programming language that has similarities to Javascript and C. Like objects in object-oriented programming, each contract contains state variables, functions, and standard data types. Contract-specific features include modifier (guard) clauses, event notifiers for listeners, and custom global variables. In the Ethereum ecosystem, Solidity is used to create contracts for voting, crowdfunding, blind auctions, multi-signature wallets, and more.

Before writing any Solidity, you need to mention to the compiler the version of Solidity it's going to use. An example is discussed below:

```
pragma solidity ^0.4.19;
```

Object-oriented programming languages have classes and solidity has contracts. Contracts are similar to classes in object-oriented programming languages. The fundamental building block of an Ethereum app is known as Contract, which contains all the variables and functions. The procedure for creating a Contract is mentioned below.

```
contract Contract1 {
}
```

Here, the contract name is FirstContract. Every content between the curly braces is the body of the contract. Nothing is in the body of the contract (what it's going to do or what code it will run). But word of contract marks it as a contract in the code, much in the same way the word object or function would in JavaScript.

Blockchain contains state variables which are stored in contract storage. Every contract has its storage. They're stored in memory with javascript variables. With state variables, they're stored on the blockchain. Pretty darn cool. We can create a string variable, name it firstVariable, and place it inside our first contract:

```
contract Contract1 {
      string Variable1;
}
```

Uint is an unsigned integer data type. The idea of signed and unsigned variables is present in solidity. Signed variables can have any value be it positive or negative. But an unsigned integer must have only a positive value. It can't be negative.

```
contract Contract1 {
      uint Uint1;
}
```

Solidity also has functions. Functions are blocks of code to be executed. A function declaration in Solidity has to be written like this:

```
function Function1(string Param1, string Param2) {
}
```

A declared function tells the compiler about a function's name and its parameters and so on. We have only scratched the surface of the Solidity programming language to construct our token in the next section. For detailed documentation on the Solidity programming, please refer to the below link.

http://solidity.readthedocs.io/en/v0.4.21/index.html

Smart Contract

Smart contracts are the pieces of code that live on the blockchain and are designed to execute commands exactly how they were instructed to. They are also capable of reading other contracts, making decisions, sending Ethereum, and executing other contracts. Thus contracts will exist and run as long as the whole network exists and will only stop in scenarios such as if they run out of gas or if they were programmed to self-destruct.

What Can You Do with Contracts? Almost anything can be done. Here, let's do some simple things. You will get funds through crowdfunding that, if successful, it will supply a radically transparent and democratic organization. This organization will only obey its citizens and will neither swerve away from its constitution nor can it be censored or shut down. And all that can be achieved in less than 300 lines of code.

Now let's apply the same concept to LUCKY DOG. We will develop a small application flow using the smart contract with Solidity. The concrete flow of implementation is as follows:

- Setting up the development environment
- Creating the Truffle project using the Truffle Box
- Making the description of the Smart Contract
- Compiling and Migrating the Smart Contract
- Testing the Smart Contract
- Creating the UI attached to the Smart Contract
- Using the DAPP with browser

Creating a Truffle Project

Let's set the environment that can use "node" and "npm."

If the OS is Debien GNU, you can install the recommended version of node.js 8.x as follows.

```
$ apt-get update
$ curl -sL https://deb.nodesource.com/setup_8.x | bash -
$ apt-get install -y nodejs
```

To start with, the Truffle has to be installed.

```
$ npm install -g truffle
```

Thus we can say that Truffle is a development framework of Ethereum which is one of the most useful frameworks for smart contract development. Here compiling and deploying the source code can be done efficiently. You will have to create a directory called "pet-shop-example" and work in this directory. Normally, initialization is done with truffle init. Firstly, an empty project has to be created. For this tutorial, let's develop it from a well-known project "Truffle Box." You can find more details on truffle box here.

https://truffle-box.github.io/

```
$ mkdir pet-shop-example
$ cd pet-shop-example
$ truffle unbox pet-shop
```

Then, the following files and directory structure is prepared inside the pet-shop-example (Fig. 6.8).

The directories and files that are used are mentioned below.

- contracts directory: This contains the source files of solidity describing the Smart Contract
- migrations directory: migration system used when deploying the Smart Contract
- test directory: Test files that are written in Javascript and Solidity
- truffle.js: Configuration file for Truffle

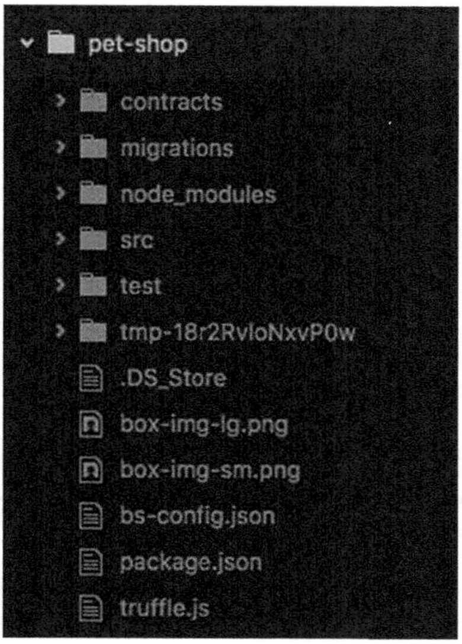

Fig. 6.8 Truffle project

Creating the Smart Contract

Create a file called "Adoption.sol" in the created contracts directory and write the following.

```
pragma solidity ^0.4.4;
 contract Adoption {
  address[16] public adopters;
 function adopt(uint petId) public returns(uint) {
   require(petId >= 0 && petId <= 15);

   adopters[petId] = msg.sender;
   return petId;
  }

 function getAdopters() public returns (address[16]) {
   return adopters;
  }
 }
```

Let's look at each part, in turn, specifying the version of the solidity compiler. Also, solidity adds a semicolon (;) at the end of the line like javascript.

```
pragma solidity ^0.4.4;
```

I declare a contract named Adoption. I will implement the contract in this.

```
contract Adoption {
 . . .
 }
```

Here "adopters" which is a state variable is declared. Since solidity is a static language, declaring the data type of the variable is required. A unique data type "address" exists in Solidity in addition to general data types such as string and uint. The address of the account is stored in "Address." Here address is an array, and 16 addresses will be present in the variable called "adopters." As the address is described as public before the "adopters" variable, it can be viewed by anyone who has access to that contract.

```
address[16] public adopters;
```

After declaring the variable like this, I declare the method of the contract.

```
function adopt(uint petId) public returns (uint) {
  require(petId >= 0 && petId <= 15);
  adopters[petId] = msg.sender;
  return petId;
 }
```

The variable "**petId**" which is an integer type is set to 0 to 15 based on the array length of adopters. (Array starts with the index of 0.) So I use require () for making petID 0 through 15.

msg.sender signifies the address of the person that called this function.

So "**adopters [petId] = msg.sender;**" adds the caller's address to the adopters array.

And **petId** is returned to the caller as the response.

With the help of the adopt function mentioned above, it's now possible to return one address, since petId is the key of adopters array.

However, since 16 API calls in every reload are required to be done, I will return the whole adopters array with the following getAdopters function.

```
function getAdopters() public returns (address[16]) {
  return adopters;
 }
```

The variable "adopters" has already been declared. Hence the data type needs to be specified, and the return value has to be returned. So this was the Smart Contract. To summarize the contents, I have created the below-mentioned Adoption contracts. Compiling and migrating this Smart Contract needs to be continued.

Compile the Smart Contract

This is the process where the source code that is written in the programming language is translated into a machine language. The computer can directly execute this machine language. In other words, it will convert the code written in the solidity language into bytecode. Thus the Ethereum Virtual Machine which is the virtual machine of Ethereum will be able to execute it. In the directory containing DAPP, launch Truffle Develop at the terminal, and so on.

```
$ truffle develop
```

Then enter "compile" at the started truffle develop console.

```
$ truffle(develop)> compile
```

If the compilation is successful, the following output will be displayed.

```
Compiling ./contracts/Adoption.sol...
 Compiling ./contracts/Migrations.sol...
 Writing artifacts to ./build/contracts
```

Though there will be a warning, which is public, it is fine to go through. (Let's keep the truffle develop console open all the time.)

Migration

It means moving an existing system or the like to a new platform. In this case, the file that is being migrated will do the deployment of the created Adoption contract to the blockchain network of Ethereum. If we look at the migrations directory, there should already be a javascript migration file called "1_initial_migration.js." Migrations.sol is deployed by this file in the contracts directory and managed so that a series of smart contracts can be migrated correctly.

Create a migration file named "2_deploy_contracts.js" in the migrations directory. In the migration file, write as follows.

```
const Adoption = artifacts.require("Adoption");
module.exports = (deployer) => {
   deployer.deploy(Adoption);
 };
```

Let's run the migrate command on the running truffle develop console.

```
$ truffle(develop)> migrate
```

And it will be successful if the below-mentioned output is done.

```
Running migration: 1_initial_migration.js
Deploying Migrations...
 ... 0xa1f5bc4affc464999763799648db42acae31772140af652d27f921ee11c
b330d
  Migrations: 0x8cdaf0cd259887258bc13a92c0a6da92698644c0
Saving successful migration to network...
  ... 0xd7bc86d31bee32fa3988f1c1eabce403a1b5d570340a3a9cdba53a472e
e8c956
Saving artifacts...
Running migration: 2_deploy_contracts.js
  Deploying Adoption...
  ... 0xe46e604dce4322e0492be99b5d3744468e20f8a233e3da551dd42ad927
2839b9
  Adoption: 0x345ca3e014aaf5dca488057592ee47305d9b3e10
Saving successful migration to network...
  ... 0xf36163615f41ef7ed8f4a8f192149a0bf633fe1a2398ce001bf44c43dc
7bdda0
Saving artifacts...
```

With this, a Smart Contract can be created, compiled, and deployed in the test block chain of the local environment. Next, let's test whether this works correctly.

Testing the Smart Contract

Testing the Smart Contract is one of the most important steps. This is because design mistakes and bugs in smart contracts are related to the user's tokens (assets), which can cause severe damage to users. The smart contract conducts two different tests. This includes the manual test and the automatic test. Let's check the operation both manually and automatically.

In the case of the manual test, the operation of the application is checked by using tools of a local development environment such as Ganache. These are easy to understand as they refer to transactions in the GUI. In Truffle, the automatic test of the Smart Contract can be described in both javascript and Solidity, but here we will use Solidity.

In the created test directory, create a file called "TestAdoption.sol" and write the following.

```
pragma solidity ^0.4.11;
 import "truffle/Assert.sol";
 import "truffle/DeployedAddresses.sol";
 import "../contracts/Adoption.sol";
contract TestAdoption {
   Adoption adoption = Adoption(DeployedAddresses.Adoption());

  function testUserCanAdoptPet() {
     uint returnedId = adoption.adopt(8);
     uint expected = 8;
     Assert.equal(returnedId, expected, "Adoption of pet ID 8
should be recorded.");
  }

 function testGetAdopterAddressByPetId() {
     address expected = this;
     address adopter = adoption.adopters(8);
     Assert.equal(adopter, expected, "Owner of pet ID 8 should
be recorded.");
  }

 function testGetAdopterAddressByPetIdInArray() {
     address expected = this;
     address[16] memory adopters = adoption.getAdopters();
     Assert.equal(adopters[8], expected, "Owner of pet ID 8
should be recorded.");
  }
}
```

It's a bit long, but let's look at it after disassembling.

```
pragma solidity ^0.4.11;
 import "truffle/Assert.sol";
 import "truffle/DeployedAddresses.sol";
 import "../contracts/Adoption.sol";
contract TestAdoption {
  Adoption adoption = Adoption(DeployedAddresses.Adoption());
  /*
  *Add a function described later here
  */
 }
```

At first, let's import the three contracts mentioned below.

Assert.sol: This includes the various checking works during testing.

DeployedAddresses.sol: Here the address of the contract deployed at the test time is obtained.

Adoption.sol: Test the Smart Contract.

Create a contract called "**TestAdoption**" and declare the variable adoption. "**adoption**" contains "**DeployedAddresses.**"

In the TestAdoption contract below, let's define the functions used for testing.

```
function testUserCanAdoptPet() {
  uint returnedId = adoption.adopt(8);
  uint expected = 8;
  Assert.equal(returnedId, expected, "Adoption of pet ID 8
should be recorded.");
 }
```

Let's test the adopt () function defined in the Adoption Contract. If the adopt () function is functioning correctly, it will return the same petId (return value) as the number of the argument.

In this case, put petId of 8 into the adopt () function and make sure it matches the return value petId with Assert.equal ().

```
function testGetAdopterAddressByPetId() {
  address expected = this;
  address adopter = adoption.adopters(8);
  Assert.equal(adopter, expected, "Owner of pet ID 8 should be
recorded.");
 }
```

Let's check whether the correct owner's address is associated with petId. We will test whether the owner's address with pet ID 8 is correct. By the way, the variable "this" represents the address in the current contract.

```
function testGetAdopterAddressByPetIdInArray() {
   address expected = this;
   address[16] memory adopters = adoption.getAdopters();
   Assert.equal(adopters[8], expected, "Owner of pet ID 8
should be recorded.");
 }
```

Finally, we have to check whether the array "adopters" that contain all the addresses that are returned correctly. The "memory" attribute is not saved in the "storage" of the contract. This means that it is a temporarily recorded value. Now that we can write the test let's run this test file with Truffle Develop.

```
$ truffle(develop)> test
```

We have successfully tested when the following output is displayed.

```
Using network 'develop.'
 Compiling ./contracts/Adoption.sol...
 Compiling ./test/TestAdoption.sol...
 Compiling truffle/Assert.sol...
 Compiling truffle/DeployedAddresses.sol...
TestAdoption

    ✓ testUserCanAdoptPet (133ms)
     ✓ testGetAdopterAddressByPetId (112ms)
     ✓ testGetAdopterAddressByPetIdInArray (196ms)

  3 passing (1s)
```

Develop the User Interface

So far, we have created the Smart Contract which is deployed in the test blockchain of the local environment and tested whether it usually works. Next, let's make a user interface where we can see pet shops on the browser. Truffle Box makes the basic structure. So now you will have to add a characteristic function in Ethereum.

The src directory is the front-end part of the application, and you will edit the /src/js/app.js file in it.

```
App = {
  web3Provider: null,
  contracts: {},
 init: function() {
   // Load pets.
   $.getJSON('../pets.json', function(data) {
    var. petsRow = $('#petsRow');
    var. petTemplate = $('#petTemplate');

   for (i = 0; i < data.length; i ++) {
      petTemplate.find('.panel-title').text(data[i].name);
      petTemplate.find('img').attr('src', data[i].picture);
      petTemplate.find('.pet-breed').text(data[i].breed);
      petTemplate.find('.pet-age').text(data[i].age);
      petTemplate.find('.pet-location').text(data[i].location);
      petTemplate.find('.btn-adopt').attr('data-id', data[i].id);

      petsRow.append(petTemplate.html());
   }
  });

  return App.initWeb3();
  },

 initWeb3: function() {
 /*
 *①Add code here
 */
   return App.initContract();
  },

 initContract: function() {
 /*
 * ②Add code here
 */
   return App.bindEvents();
  },

 bindEvents: function() {
   $(document).on('click', '.btn-adopt', App.handleAdopt);
  },
```

```
markAdopted: function(adopters, account) {
/*
* ③Add code here
*/
 },
 handleAdopt: function(event) {
  event.preventDefault();
  var petId = parseInt($(event.target).data('id'));
/*
* ④Add code here
*/
 }
};

$(function() {
 $(window).load(function() {
  App.init();
  });
});
```

Installation of Web 3

First, you will have to make sure if the instance of web3 is "active." If it is "active," it will be replaced with the web3 object of the created application. If it's not "active," create a web3 object in the local development environment.

```
if (typeof web3 !== 'undefined') {
   App.web3Provider = web3.currentProvider;
 } else {
   App.web3Provider = new Web3.providers.HttpProvider('http://
localhost:9545');
 }
 web3 = new Web3(App.web3Provider);
```

Instantiation of Contract

Since communicating with "Ethereum Network" via web 3 is possible, the "Smart Contract" that is created will be instantiated. For achieving that, we need to tell web 3 where the contract is and how it works.

```
$.getJSON('Adoption.json', function(data) {
  var AdoptionArtifact = data;
  App.contracts.Adoption = TruffleContract(AdoptionArtifact);
  App.contracts.Adoption.setProvider(App.web3Provider);
  return App.markAdopted();
});
```

"Truffle contract" is a useful library of Truffle. This is a library on web3, which makes it easy to connect with "contract." For example, the truffle contract synchronizes the contract information during migration, so you do not need to change the deployed address manually. The Artifact file comprises the information on the deployed address and ABI (Application Binary Interface). Information is represented by ABI on the interface, that is, the variable, function, parameter, and so on, of the contract.

Insert Artifact into the TruffleContract() function and instantiate the contract. Then set the App.web3Provider created by instantiating web3 to its contract.

UI Update

Let's make sure that the state of the pet kept changed, and the UI is updated. First, getAdopters () is called on an instance of the deployed Adoption contract. The call () function does not change the state of the blockchain. It reads the data, so you do not need to pay gas. And check whether each petId is tied to an address. If an address exists, change the button to success so that you cannot press the button.

```
var adoptionInstance;
  App.contracts.Adoption.deployed().then(function(instance) {
   adoptionInstance = instance;
   return adoptionInstance.getAdopters.call();
  }).then(function(adopters) {
  for (i = 0; i < adopters.length; i++) {
   if (adopters[i] !== '0x0000000000000000000000000000000000000
   0000') {
    $('panel-pet').eq(i).find('button').text('Success').attr
('disabled', true);
  }
  }
  }).catch(function(err) {
   console.log(err.message);
  });
```

Manipulating the Adopt Function

In this case, after confirming the error of the account using web 3, we will process the actual transaction. The adopt () function does transaction execution, and it takes an object containing the address of petId and the account as an argument.

Then, the transaction execution result will be reflected in the UI as the new data.

```
var adoptionInstance;
 web3.eth.getAccounts(function(error, accounts) {
  if (error) {
    console.log(error);
  }
  var account = accounts[0];
  App.contracts.Adoption.deployed().then(function(instance) {
    adoptionInstance = instance;
    return adoptionInstance.adopt(petId, {from: account});
  }).then(function(result) {
    return App.markAdopted();
  }).catch(function(err) {
    console.log(err.message);
  });
 });
```

Now if you are ready to use DAPP, let's use the created DAPP in your browser!

Completion of the Application

We will use MetaMask which is the extension of Chrome. During that time, the account will use the account for Truffle Develop by using the following Wallet Seed. This Seed is displayed when Truffle Develop is executed. (It is common seed.)candy maple cake sugar pudding cream honey rich smooth crumble sweet treat

(If you are using MetaMask now you can go from the menu Lock to the following screen.) (Fig. 6.9).

The MetaMask has to be connected to the blockchain created by the Truffle Develop. To achieve that, you will have to change it from "Main Network" on the upper left to "Custom RPC." And let's change to http://localhost:9545 for "Truffle Develop." The display changes from "Main Network" to "Private Network" (Fig. 6.10).

Fig. 6.9 Metamask wallet

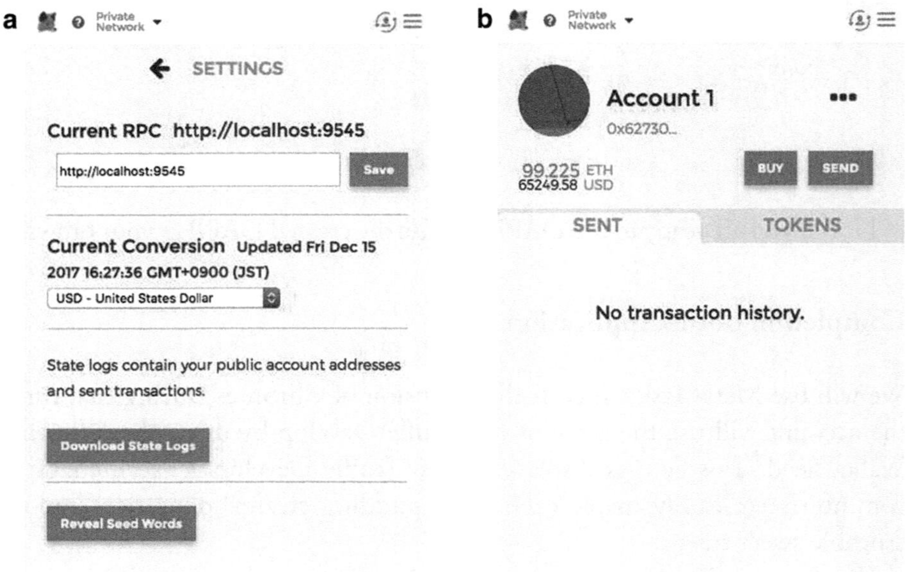

Fig. 6.10 (a) Connecting to the Ethereum network. (b) Metamask accounts

Accounts that are made from the seed mentioned above have weak 100ETH. It is drawn by the amount of gas consumed in the contract deployment. Firstly, you will have to set up the MetaMask as it has been stated above. Then the local web server can be started by executing the following code in terminal, (The lite - server library can be used, since bs - config.json and package.json have been created.)

```
$ npm run dev
```

Then, DAPP like the one shown below can be displayed on the browser (Fig. 6.11).

If the "adopt" button of your favorite pet is clicked, the transaction is sent by "MetaMask," and then you can purchase pets by ETH payment! (Fig. 6.12).

Fig. 6.11 Browser display

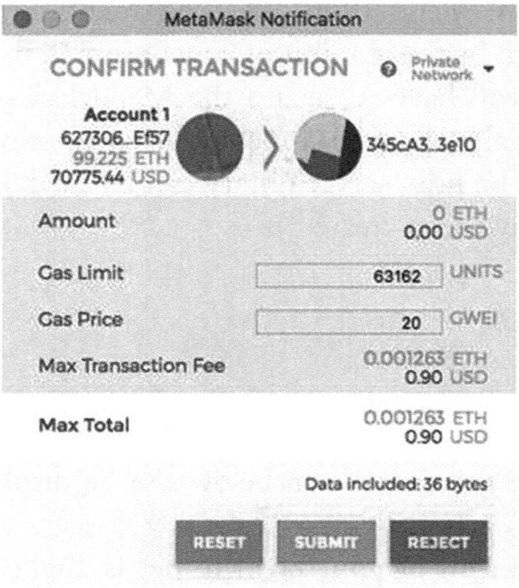

Fig. 6.12 Adopt payment processing

Create an ERC 20 Token on Ethereum

A specific set of functions known as ERC20 are required by the developers to use in their tokens to make them ERC20 compliant. This is not an enforced rule. To make their tokens undergo interactions with various wallets, exchanges, and smart contracts without any issues, most developers involved in developing DAPP are encouraged to follow the standards. This gave everyone an idea of how future tokens are expected to behave. ERC20 tokens have gotten widespread approval, and most of the DAPPS sold on initial coin offerings (ICOs) have tokens based on the ERC20 standard.

We are familiar with ICOs by now. Investors invest millions of dollars in many projects that promise a revolutionary technology through smart contracts. It will change the world. Most of the time there is only that, a promise, along with a white paper and a website and the MVP is developed after the crowd sale. In this section, we'll demonstrate how easy it is actually to make your own ERC20 token for the Ethereum blockchain.

Now, let's revisit the LUCKY token that we discussed in Chap. 4 and try to build it on the Ethereum blockchain. To give a quick recap, the LUCKY coin is a utility token used in the business of Dog care. Figure 6.13 illustrates the Lucky coin marketplace.

LUCKY coin is a blockchain venture with the goal of revolutionizing the dog world through blockchain technology. The platform is set to offer its LUCKY ERC20 token for use in its global ecosystem of pet care. The crypto

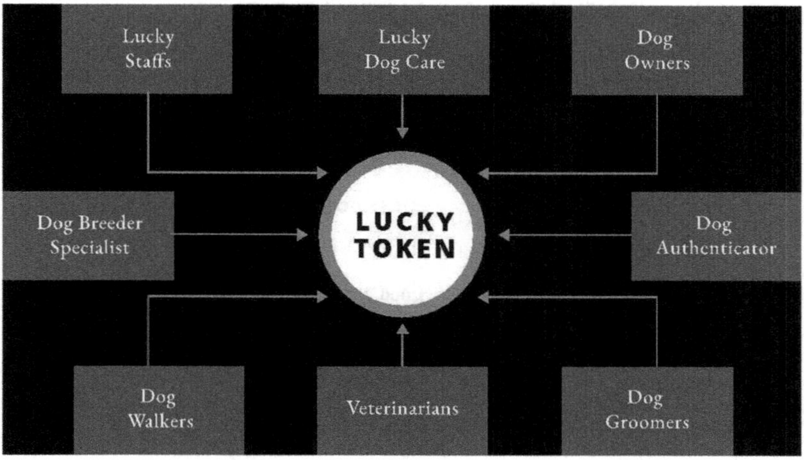

Fig. 6.13 Lucky coin marketplace

currency will facilitate dog care services and data management between pet owners, veterinarians, dog insurers, dog breeders, dog authenticators, dog walkers, dog groomers, and many other participants. As the first crypto for the dog world, LUCKY coin plans to introduce a reward program that will inspire participation across the world of dog owners. Each dog owner or veterinarian who makes a contribution that will benefit the LUCKY coin ecosystem will receive a reward through a transparent and decentralized reward scheme.

LUCKY Coin: Decentralized Pet Care Blockchain Solution Features

With the objective of improving the worldwide health care of dogs, **LUCKY coin** plans to initiate this through three features on its platform. The first feature is the dog assurance concept. In this, the dog owner has the option to ensure his or her pet with a blockchain-based insurance scheme that is aligned to suit their dog's needs. Each insurance cover will be rated on the basis of the health condition of the pets and aligned to the dog's veterinarian.

A health database will protect pet health records and data in a decentralized database. The pet owner or the veterinarian will have access to the information ecosystem through special permission. If the pet owners want to keep up with post-treatment or monitoring of their dog's health condition, they can do so through an aftercare mobile app. The application will be made available to the Android operating system to achieve the platform's goal of a global pet world.

ERC 20 Token Definition for LUCKY DOG

For creating an ERC20 token, you need the following:

	Description	Value
1.	Token Name	LUCKY DOG
2.	Token Symbol	LUCKY
3.	Intial Supply	1,000,000
4.	Total Supply	1,000,000
5.	Max Supply	1,000,000
6.	Decimal Units	0
7.	Version	1.0

The decimal places are where things can get tricky. Most tokens have 18 decimal places. It means that you can have up to 0.0000000000000000001 tokens. When creating the token, you'll have to keep in mind the decimal places you'd like and how it should fit into the larger picture of your project. For illustration, let's keep it simple such that either the people will have a token or they won't have one. We are not keeping anything in between. So, let's choose 0. But you could choose 1 if you wanted people to have half a token, or 18 if you wanted it to be "standard."

Token Smart Contract Specification

Let's define specific roles for the token maintenance purposes.

Creator—Person who develops and deploys the Smart Contract (Development Team).

Administrator—Person who maintains the business. In our case, Mark or his immediate subordinate will become the admin as this will be the highest level of control on the Smart Contract behavior.

Let's now lay down some ground rules for our token contract to prepare a spec.

1. The coin must be called LUCKY DOG and must have the symbol as LUCKY.
2. The creator must be able to specify the initial supply, total supply, max supply, and decimal units during the creation.
3. Users must be able to transfer the coins to each other's account.
4. Any debt or negative balance should not be allowed.
5. There should be one administrator who may not be the currency creator. That is, the currency creator must make someone as admin during the creation.

6. Anyone must be able to buy or sell the LUCKY using Ethereums.
7. Buy or sell price must be set by Admin at any time.
8. Admin must be able to transfer the administrator role to any other address.
9. Admin must be able to mint the new LUCKY to anyone's address.
10. Admin must be able to freeze or unfreeze the coins of anyone's account.
11. Admin must be able to set up a spender account with an allowance limit.

Now that we have a token definition and a Smart Contract specification let's get started with some coding.

Minimum Viable Token

We will create a digital token. Coins, loyalty points, gold certificates, IOUs, in-game items, and so on, are the fungible tradable goods that can be represented by tokens in the Ethereums ecosystem. All tokens implement some essential features in a standard way. Your token and the Ethereums wallet will be instantly compatible with each other. I will also be compatible with any other client or contract that uses the same standards.

The standard token contract can be quite complicated. A very basic token boils down to this (Fig. 6.14):

Breaking down the code into its bare necessities may give you a clear picture. There are three specific parts of this function:

- The mapping.
- Giving the creator all the tokens.
- Transferring the token to a sender for Ethereum.

```
pragma solidity ^0.4.20;

contract LuckyDog {
  /* This creates an array with all balances */
   mapping (address => uint256) public balanceOf;

  /* Initializes contract with initial supply tokens to the creator of the contract */
  function LuckyDog(
      uint256 initialSupply
    ) public {
      balanceOf[msg.sender] = initialSupply;          // Give the creator all initial tokens
  }

  /* Send coins */
  function transfer(address _to, uint256 _value) public {
      require(balanceOf[msg.sender] >= _value);        // sender's has enough coin to send
      require(balanceOf[_to] + _value >= balanceOf[_to]); // Make sure there is no overflow
      balanceOf[msg.sender] -= _value;               // deduct the amout from sender's balance
      balanceOf[_to] += _value;                 // add the corresponding amount to the recipient
  }
}
```

Fig. 6.14 Minimum viable token

The Mapping In this part, the mapping will be done. Here a database is created where everyone will be able to view your token balance. Tokens like ETH are logged into an open ledger. All the balances and transactions relating to that particular token will be visible to everyone.

```
contract LuckyDog {
  /* This creates an array with all balances */
   mapping (address => uint256) public balanceOf;
```

Giving the Creator All the Tokens In this part of the function, whoever has created the smart contract and tokens will get all the tokens:

```
/* Initializes contract with initial supply tokens to the creator of the contract */
   function LuckyDog(
        uint256 initialSupply
      ) public {
        balanceOf[msg.sender] = initialSupply;          // Give the creator all initial tokens
   }
```

Transfer the Token to a Sender for Ethereum Finally, we reached the last part of the code. An equivalent amount of token can be made available to the sender for the Ethereum that they invest into the DAPP.

```
   /* Send coins */
   function transfer(address _to, uint256 _value) public {
        require(balanceOf[msg.sender] >= _value);        // sender's has enough coin to send
        require(balanceOf[_to] + _value >= balanceOf[_to]); // Make sure there is no overflow
        balanceOf[msg.sender] -= _value;            // deduct the amout from sender's balance
        balanceOf[_to] += _value;              // add the corresponding amount to the recipient
   }
```

Transfer logic is very self-explanatory. It first checks the sender's available balance of the tokens. Then it deducts the said amount from the sender's balance and then credits that value to the recipient's balance.

Complete Token Contract for the LUCKY DOG is available in Appendix A.

Create an ICO (Crowd Sale) Contract on Ethereum

The process of crowdfunding includes raising funds for a project or venture from the masses. This is a place where to generate a large investment people make investments in smaller amounts. This investment is used to meet the requirements. The investment plan is distributed across the masses. This is done to prevent any single person from spending more than he can spare. Also, there are instances where artists, authors, philosophers have crowdfunded their works.

Blockchain technology manages the value exchange under contract. This feature will come handy when it comes to managing rewards-based and equity-based crowdfunding campaigns. Automation of the whole process of assigning relevant rewards and equity against their contributions is possible by using blockchain-based smart contracts for crowdfunding. A set of predefined crowdfunding conditions is programmed on smart contracts. The system can be automated so that the smart contract is executed. The objective of this is issuing certain rewards or proof of ownership of a certain percentage of equity that is based on the amount contributed toward the campaign.

Crowd sales are a kind of crowdfunding campaigns in the crypto currency world. Here the premined crypto tokens for the platform under development are sold using the digital currency platform by exchanging Bitcoin, Ethereum, or some other established digital currency. The raised funds are then used for further developing the platform. The crypto tokens bought by the participants of the crowd sale are equivalent to both rewards and equity (depending upon the model followed by the platform). Blockchain technology and digital currencies have proven to be capable of being retrofitted to meet the needs of any industry, including the time-tested ones. Crowdfunding is one such segment, into which the technology is capable of blending in, entirely. Let's build the crowd sale contract for the LUCKY coin using Solidity.

LUCKY Token contract definition

	Description	Value
1.	Ether price for LUCKY (ETH)	0.001
2.	Minimum ETH required to buy LUCKY	1
3.	Funding Minimum Target (ETH)	1000
4.	Funding Minimum Target (ETH) - Soft Cap	5000
5.	Funding Minimum Target (ETH) - Hard Cap	10000
6.	Total Raised (ETH)	
7.	Current Balance (ETH)	
8.	Crowd Sale/Lucky website	https://luckydog.io
9.	Beneficiary Account Address	<Beneficiary Account's Address>
10.	Duration of Crowd Sale	240h
11.	Crowd Sale Completed At	<Date and Time of completion>

ICO Smart Contract Specification

1. CrowdSale smart contract for LUCKY must be able to initialize the following:
    - Ethereum price for LUCKY (ETH)
    - Minimum ETH required to buy LUCKY
    - Funding Minimum Target (ETH)
    - Funding Maximum Target (ETH)—Soft Cap
    - Funding Maximum Target (ETH)—Hard Cap
    - Crowd Sale/LuckyDog website
    - Beneficiary Account Address
    - Duration of Crowd sale
2. Crowd Sale smart contract should maintain a state that will indicate one of the following:
    - Fund-raising
    - Failed
    - Successful
    - Closed
3. Provide a function to pay ETH and buy LUCKY tokens
4. Should maintain a list of contributor address and the amount contributed in ETH
5. Provide properties to view the total amount of ETH raised so far and the current balance of the ETH
6. Check the status of the funding after each contribution
7. If the status reaches the required maximum limit, then perform the payout to the beneficiary account and trigger the end of the LifeCycle event
8. If the status is InComplete and Expired, then execute the refund logic to send back the contributed ETH and trigger the end of the LifeCycle event
9. Perform necessary validations and log all events

The way this particular crowd sale contract works is that you will have to set an exchange rate for your token. A proportional amount of tokens in exchange of their Ethereum will immediately be available to the donors. A funding goal and a deadline will also have to be set. Once that deadline is over, you can ping the contract, and if the goal were reached, it would send the Ethereum raised to you. Otherwise, it goes back to the donors. Donors keep their tokens even if the project doesn't achieve its goal, as a proof that they helped. Below is the complete crowd sale contract that we are going to use for LUCKY DOG project (Fig. 6.15).

ICO Smart Contract Code

```
pragma solidity ^0.4.16;

interface token {
  function transfer(address receiver, uint amount);
}

contract Crowdsale {
    address public beneficiary;
    uint public fundingGoal;
    uint public amountRaised;
    uint public deadline;
    uint public price;
    token public tokenReward;
    mapping(address => uint256) public balanceOf;
    bool fundingGoalReached = false;
    bool crowdsaleClosed = false;

   event GoalReached(address recipient, uint totalAmountRaised);
   event FundTransfer(address backer, uint amount, bool isContribution);

   /**
    * Constructor function
    *
    * Setup the owner
    */
   function Crowdsale(
        address ifSuccessfulSendTo,
        uint fundingGoalInEthers,
        uint durationInMinutes,
        uint etherCostOfEachToken,
        address addressOfTokenUsedAsReward
   ){
        beneficiary = ifSuccessfulSendTo;
        fundingGoal = fundingGoalInEthers * 1 ether;
        deadline = now + durationInMinutes * 1 minutes;
        price = etherCostOfEachToken * 1 ether;
        tokenReward = token(addressOfTokenUsedAsReward);
   }

   /**
    * Fallback function
    *
    * The function without name is the default function that is called whenever anyone sends funds to a contract
    */
   function () payable {
        require(!crowdsaleClosed);
        uint amount = msg.value;
        balanceOf[msg.sender] += amount;
        amountRaised += amount;
        tokenReward.transfer(msg.sender, amount / price);
        FundTransfer(msg.sender, amount, true);
   }

    modifier afterDeadline() { if (now >= deadline) _; }

   /**
    * Check if goal was reached
    *
    * Checks if the goal or time limit has been reached and ends the campaign
    */
   function checkGoalReached() afterDeadline {
     if (amountRaised >= fundingGoal){
          fundingGoalReached = true;
          GoalReached(beneficiary, amountRaised);
     }
        crowdsaleClosed = true;
   }


   /**
    * Withdraw the funds
    *
    * Checks to see if goal or time limit has been reached, and if so, and the funding goal was reached,
    * sends the entire amount to the beneficiary. If goal was not reached, each contributor can withdraw
    * the amount they contributed.
    */
```

```
function safeWithdrawal() afterDeadline {
  if (!fundingGoalReached) {
      uint amount = balanceOf[msg.sender];
      balanceOf[msg.sender] = 0;
    if (amount > 0) {
      if (msg.sender.send(amount)) {
           FundTransfer(msg.sender, amount, false);
      } else {
           balanceOf[msg.sender] = amount;
      }
    }
  }

  if (fundingGoalReached && beneficiary == msg.sender) {
    if (beneficiary.send(amountRaised)) {
        FundTransfer(beneficiary, amountRaised, false);
    } else {
      //If send fails, unlock funders balance
        fundingGoalReached = false;
    }
  }
 }
}
```

ICO Smart Contract Flow Diagram

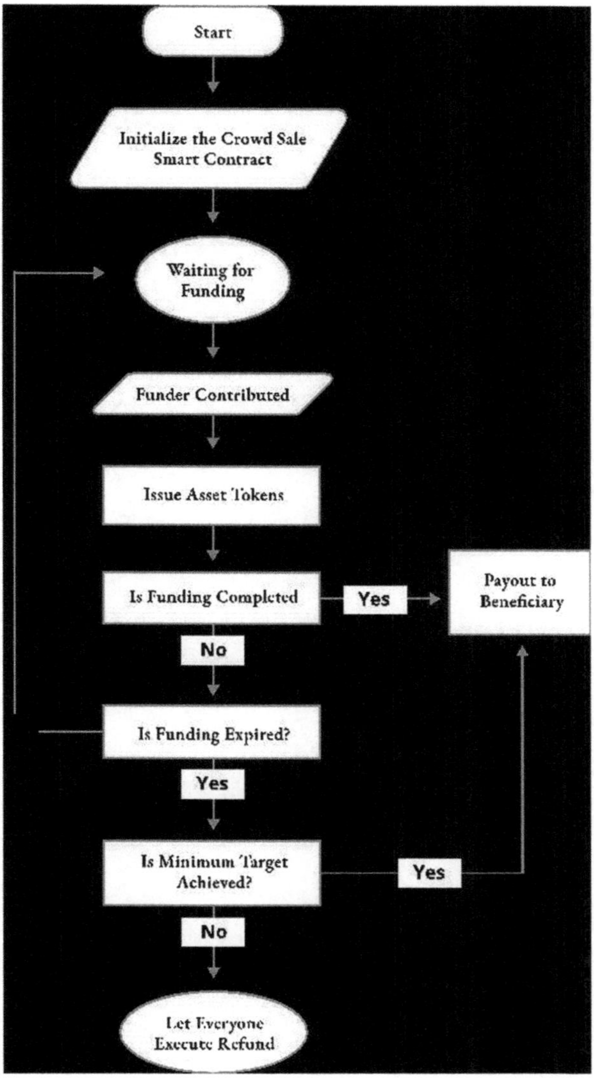

Fig. 6.15 ICO smart contract flow diagram

7

Creation of a Distributed Ledger

Sarah Swammy, Richard Thompson, and Marvin Loh

Blockchain

Over the last few years the words blockchain, Bitcoin, and mining have been buzzing around all over the internet. Before we jump right into the details of crypto currency, I want to explain these buzzwords, which will help us absorb the later sections with much more clarity. Blockchain is a continuously growing list of records called blocks. Every block in the blockchain typically contains a cryptographic hash of the previous block, a timestamp, and transaction data. Blockchain was designed so that the transactions are immutable, meddle-proof, and distributed. Figure 7.1 demonstrates a very simple visualization of a blockchain.

Let's take a little deeper insight into the blockchain and analyze it from bottom up starting from a Hash.

Hash

In modest terms, hashing is a software concept of taking an input data of any length and running it through a cryptographic algorithm and producing an output of a fixed length. A Hash is a bunch of random alphanumeric characters. It is like a fingerprint of some digital data. Let's explore how the hashing process works. We are going to put in certain inputs. Following is a set of Hash being generated for different set of data.

S. Swammy et al., *Crypto Uncovered*, https://doi.org/10.1007/978-3-030-00135-3_7

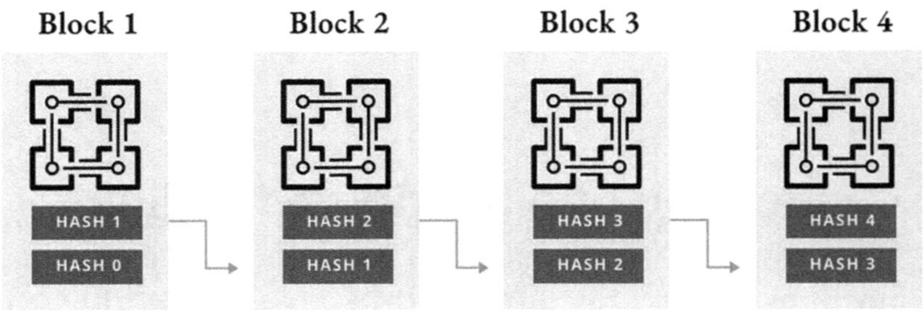

Fig. 7.1 Blockchain

Data	Hash
Hi	3639EFCD08ABB273B1619E82E78C29A7DF02C1051B1820E99FC395DC AA3326B8
Blockchain	625DA44E4EAF58D61CF048D168AA6F5E492DEA166D8BB54EC06C 30DE07DB57E1
How are you?	DF287DFC1406ED2B692E1C2C783BB5CEC97EAC53151EE1D9810397 AA0AFA0D89
Crypto currency	6EC60FE39028887E7FE9C4B025545748953C27515073BF9AD17CEB 5417A407D7

In the above examples, the input string is of variable lengths, but the output always has a fixed 256-bit length. This turns out to be even more complex when you are dealing with a huge amount of data and transactions. So basically, a hash is unique for every input, which makes it more convenient to store the hash instead of the original string wherever appropriate. The best example is password storage where the actual password string does not get stored in the database; instead, you keep just the hash of the password which makes your system more secure. Let's now analyze the internals of the hashing procedure and see how we can use it in a blockchain.

A cryptographic hash function is a complex mathematical algorithm which has certain properties which are considered to be secure.

1. Deterministic—Processing the same input multiple times always produces the same result. This is very important because if you get different hashes for multiple iterations of the same input then it will be impossible to keep track of the input.
2. Quick Computation—The hash function should be capable of returning the hash of an input quickly. If the process isn't fast enough then the system simply won't be efficient.
3. Pre-Image Resistance—For any given hash value H(A) it is infeasible to determine A, where A is the input and H(A) is the output hash.

4. Pseudorandomness—For any small change in the input, the changes that will be reflected in the hash will be huge. Let's check it out using SHA-256. The words Single and Mingle have just a one alphabet different but their hashes are completely different.

Single	8888A029AAF60B70574640EFD1655343D1C46C692918C113C16F44F606477253
Mingle	5FB188B33D53EAD28780E22822A34CE1C624740A6F5C85C7AF0D12607EAF5D51

5. Collision Resistant—Given two different inputs X and Y where H(X) and H (Y) are their respective hashes, it is infeasible for H (X) to be equal to H(Y). So, for the most part, each input will have its own unique hash.
6. Puzzle-Friendly—For every single output "Y," if k is selected from a distribution with high min-entropy it is infeasible to determine an input x such that $H(k|x) = Y$. Assume you have an output value "Y." If you select a random value "k" from a wide distribution, it is infeasible to determine a value X to the extent that the hash of the concatenation of k and x will produce the output Y. Please note the word "infeasible," it is not impossible. In fact, the mining process works upon this.

Following are a few examples of cryptographic hash functions:

- MD 5: Produces a 128-bit hash. Collision resistance was broken after ~2^21 hashes.
- SHA 1: Produces a 160-bit hash. Collision resistance broke after ~2^61 hashes.
- SHA 256: Produces a 256-bit hash. This is currently being used by Bitcoin.
- Keccak-256: Produces a 256-bit hash and is currently used by Ethereum.

Block

A block is the most recent and current part of a blockchain, which registers some or all of the latest transactions. Once finalized, the block goes into the blockchain as a permanent catalog. Each time a block gets finalized, a new one is generated. There is an endless number of such blocks in the blockchain, linked to each other (like links in a chain) in proper linear, chronological order. Every block holds a hash of the previous block. The blockchain has comprehensive information about different user addresses and their balances right from the genesis block to the most recently finalized block. Below is a sample of a block that consists of the following properties. This is a very simplified block and is not a replica of Bitcoin.

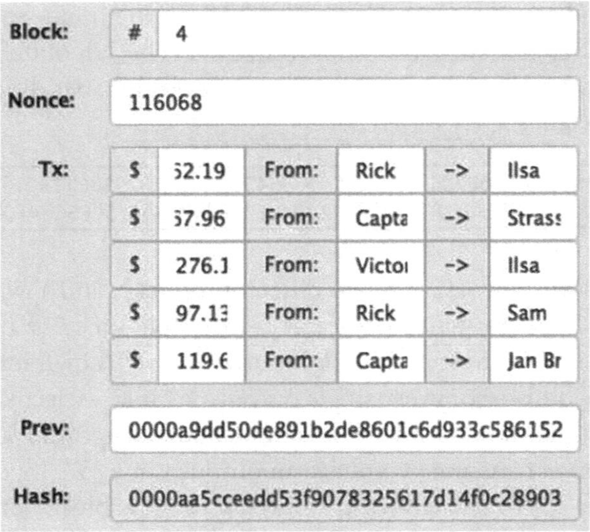

Fig. 7.2 Block structure

Block Identifier, which is a sequential number.
Nonce, which is a random number.
Tx, which is the actual transaction information.
Prev, which is the hash of the previous block.
Hash, which is the computed hash value of the data and Nonce.

As discussed in the earlier sections, every string will have its own unique hash value. Any small change in the string will have a substantial change in the value of the Hash. If you take a much closer look at the hash value in Fig. 7.2, the Hash value starts with a particular format starting with four zeros "0000," which is very uncommon and more difficult to arrive at. This pattern of the hash value in a block is achieved in the process of mining. Miners have to determine the value of the random number called the Nonce which when combined with the transaction data will result in the hash that has the patter on four leading zeros. When this hash is produced the block is considered signed. When a miner successfully signs the block before any other miner does, he or she receives the block reward and the block is added to the blockchain.

Mining

Miners enter the Bitcoin network by configuring the Bitcoin core software and building a node environment on a computer that meets minimum resource requirements. After completing the environment build, a potential

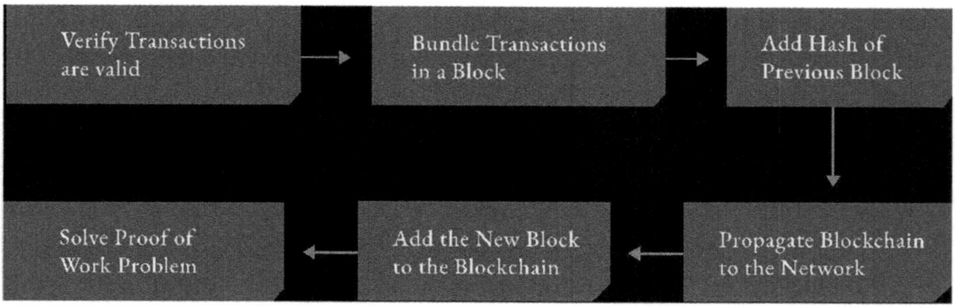

Fig. 7.3 Mining process

miner performs the initial block download that synchronizes nodes within the network downloads block and points the node to the tip of the best blockchain.

A node (computer) performing a transaction on the network has to broadcast the transaction to all the other nodes in the network. Each node in the network has to solve a mathematical problem to verify that the transaction is valid. Once verified, the node has to vote YES. At least 51% of the nodes on the network have to vote YES for the transaction to be successful. This process of verifying the transaction using distributed processing is called mining and the nodes that are involved in this verification process are called miners. The first node that verifies the transaction gets a small reward for a job well done. Figure 7.3 illustrates the mining process.

Once a Bitcoin transaction is propagated on the Bitcoin network, it does not become part of the shared ledger (the blockchain) until it is verified and included in a block in a process called mining. The Bitcoin mining process serves two purposes in Bitcoin:

- Mining generates new Bitcoins in each block, practically like a central bank printing new money. The amount of Bitcoin generated per block is fixed and diminishes with time.
- Mining generates trust by ensuring that transactions are only confirmed if enough computational power was devoted to the block that contains them. More blocks require more computation, which eventually means more trust.

The Bitcoin system of trust is fundamentally based on computation. Transactions are bundled into blocks, which requires a huge amount of computation to prove, but only a little amount of computation to verify as proven, in a process called mining. Bitcoin mining is purposely designed to be extremely resource-intensive and difficult so that the number of blocks found each day by miners remains fixed. So, a good way to describe mining is like a puzzle that resets every time somebody finds a solution and its difficulty automatically adjusts so that it takes about ten minutes to find a solution. The puzzle used in Bitcoin is developed based on a cryptographic hash, which is asymmetrically difficult to solve, but at the same time easy to verify and its difficulty can be adjusted. Finding such a solution, in blockchain terms "Proof of Work," requires millions of hashing operations per second, across the entire Bitcoin network. The algorithm for Proof of Work involves hashing the header of the block and a random number with the SHA256 cryptographic algorithm, until a solution matching a predetermined pattern emerges. The first miner who finds such a solution wins the round of competition and publishes that block into the blockchain. Every ten minutes, miners produce a new block, which comprises all the transactions since the last block. New transactions are continuously flowing into the blockchain network from user wallets and various other sources. As these transactions enter into the Bitcoin network nodes, they get collected into a temporary unverified transaction pool of each Bitcoin node. When miners build a new block of transactions, they pick the unverified transactions from this pool and then try to solve a very difficult problem (Proof of Work) to prove the validity of that new block.

Taking from where we left the previous chapter, our dinner guy, who also happens to be a miner is now sitting before his ASIC computers mining for Bitcoins. So, his computers are now trying to find the Proof of Work like thousands of others at the same time. Let's say for the sake of luck, Harry finds the solution now before others on the network. As soon as the solution is found, it validates all transactions within the block and the block is not pushed publicly to the network. All nodes now receive the new block and continue to find the Proof of Work for the next block (with the new transactions) (Fig. 7.4).

The Bitcoin mining network difficulty is the measure of how difficult it is to find a new block. It is recalculated every 2016 blocks to a value such that the previous 2016 blocks would have been generated in exactly two weeks had

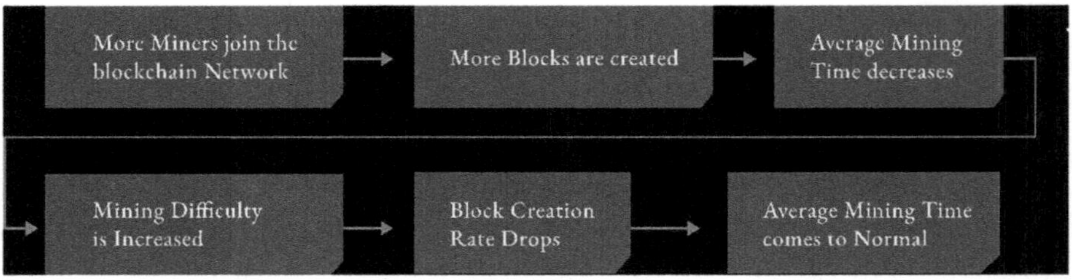

Fig. 7.4 Mining rate management

everyone been mining at this difficulty. This will yield, on average, one block every ten minutes.

Transactions get added to the new block, prioritized by the highest-paying transactions first and a few other inclusion criteria. When a miner receives a block confirmation from the network, it means they have lost the competition and must start a new block. Each miner starts constructing a new block of transactions as soon as they receive the previous block from the network and start calculating the Proof of Work for the new block. Each miner includes a special transaction in their block, one that pays their own Bitcoin address a reward of newly created Bitcoins. Currently the Bitcoin network pays about 12.5 Bitcoins per block which used to be 50 Bitcoins a couple of years back. If a miner finds a solution that makes that block valid, he or she wins this reward for the successful block that is added to the global blockchain. Bitcoin mining difficulty is a measure of how difficult it is to find a hash below the target value (Fig. 7.5).

As every new block added to the blockchain is based on the previous block added, it adds even more computation on top of that block, thereby increasing the trust in those transactions. The blocks that are mined after the one

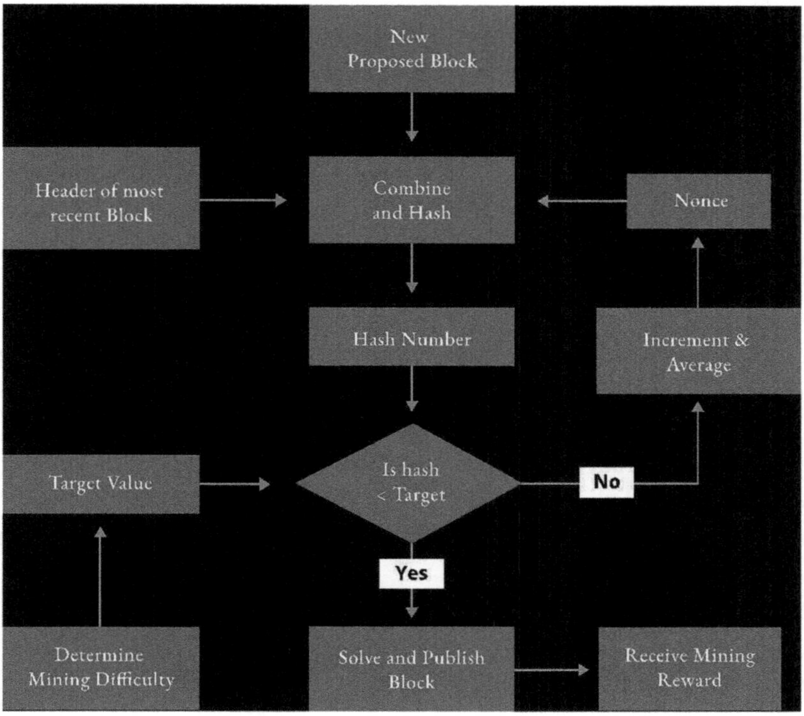

Fig. 7.5 Mining process flow

that contains your transaction act as additional assurance; as more blocks get piled up more computation is required in a longer and longer chain. Each block that is mined on top of the one containing your transaction is called one confirmation for that transaction. As more blocks get added on top of each other, it becomes exponentially difficult to reverse the transaction, thereby making it increasingly trusted by the network. By convention, any block with more than six confirmations is considered irrevocable, as it would require an enormous amount of computation to invalidate and recalculate six blocks.

Bitcoin

A strange person by the name Satoshi Nakamoto published a white paper in 2008 and explained what a blockchain would look like and explained how to run a value system on it. Subsequently he created Bitcoin as a distributed network that maintains a ledger of balances in chronological order. Anyone who has a record in this network is said to possess Bitcoins. A record in the Bitcoin ledger has an address and transactions. The address determines the identity and the transaction determines the value. As the popularity of Bitcoin started to grow more people wanted to acquire Bitcoins, and many merchants started to accept Bitcoins in place of dollars and euros. Slowly Bitcoin evolved as a currency system which runs on the internet powered by blockchain and cryptography. Satoshi Nakamoto's original paper is still recommended reading for anyone studying how Bitcoins work. Below is the link to download a copy of the Bitcoin white paper published in 2008 by Satoshi Nakamoto.

https://bitcoin.org/en/bitcoin-paper

A transaction is said to be an interaction between a user and the system. To understand it, let's take a few examples here.

Facebook: Like, Share, and Comment are a few of the social transactions between the user and the system.
Twitter: Tweet and Retweet are the basic transactions that a user makes on the system.
Github: The developer user interacts with the system via Push, Pull, Merge, and so on.
Crypto currency/Bitcoin: Send money is a transaction.

The example below illustrates how the ledger is maintained in a blockchain.

Transaction 1: Dave sends $25 to Emily at 1/1/2018 5:00 PM UTC
Transaction 2: Dave sends $15 to Joan at 1/1/2018 5:20 PM UTC
Transaction 3: Joan sends $56 to Mike at 1/1/2018 5:45 PM UTC
Transaction 4: Mike sends $35 to Emily at 1/1/2018 6:00 PM UTC

As you can notice, the transactions are added to the block in the chronological order by the time of the transaction, and all the transactions in a blockchain are immutable. This ensures that there is no way somebody can trick the system to make a double spend. Also, blockchain is a decentralized system. The banks that we have in the world are mostly running a centralized system. If the bank gets hacked or encounters financial trouble, everybody's money gets lost. Blockchain is a decentralized system, where all the nodes in the system contain the complete database of all transactions. So, in order to break down the system, at least 51% of the nodes need to be hacked, which is nearly impossible. Figure 7.6 illustrates a centralized and a decentralized system.

Bitcoin crossed 500,000 blocks during the time of writing this book. We will deal with blockchain and Bitcoin in greater depth in the next chapter. I am just scratching the surface in this chapter so that we can understand the basics of crypto currency. Bitcoin is the first crypto currency that is sustainable and publicly accepted. All other crypto currencies are called alternative coins or altcoins for short. There are more than 1000 altcoins at the time of this writing. As more and more people started buying Bitcoins, it became more expensive and difficult for people to buy one whole Bitcoin at the price of $9000 at the time of this writing. But you can also buy a satoshi which is a fraction of the Bitcoin.

$$1 \text{ Satoshi} = 0.00000001\ \text{Ƀ} = \$0.0000931607$$

In future satoshi may also become expensive, but there is a lot of time for that to happen. Let's look at the price pattern of Bitcoin during the last one year which explains when the demand started and how the value is sustained (Fig. 7.7).

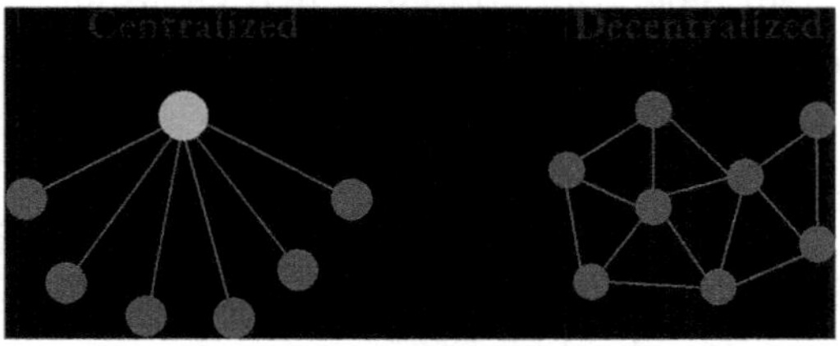

Fig. 7.6 Centralized versus decentralized system

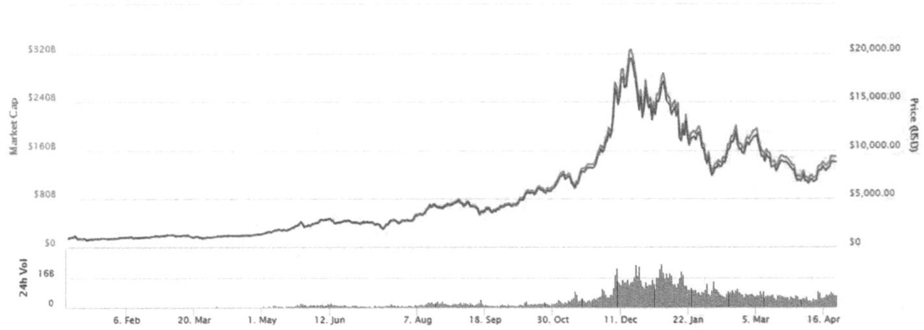

Fig. 7.7 Bitcoin price chart. (From CoinMarketCap.com)

Crypto Currency Wallet

Crypto currency wallets are software applications that store your public and private keys and interface with various blockchains and provide functionalities to check the balance, send money, and conduct other operations. When a wallet user sends Bitcoins or any other type of digital currency to you, they are basically signing off ownership of the coins to the sender's wallet address. To be able to realize the funds, the private key stored in your wallet software must match the public address the currency is attached to. If public and private keys of the sender and receiver match, the balance in your wallet software will increase, and consequently the sender's account balance will decrease. There is no actual exchange of physical coins. The transaction is implied merely by a transaction record on the blockchain and a change in balance in your crypto currency wallet (Fig. 7.8).

Let us now understand this process with an example. Let Mark be a customer who has a Bitcoin wallet and is now ready to receive funds.

- Once Mark signs up for a Bitcoin account, his wallet application will randomly generate a private key together with its corresponding Bitcoin address.
- His Bitcoin address is merely a number that corresponds to a key that he can use to control access to the funds. There is no association between that address and an account.
- Until the moment when this address is participating in a Bitcoin transaction as a sender or a receiver (recipient) of value posted on the Bitcoin ledger (the blockchain), it is simply part of the massive number of possible addresses that are valid in a Bitcoin.
- Once the address has been associated with a transaction, it becomes part of the identified addresses in the network and Mark can check his balance on the public ledger (explained later).

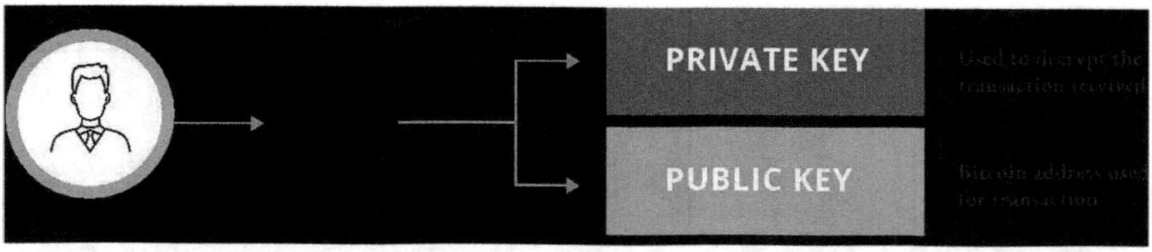

Fig. 7.8 Crypto currency wallets

Let's say Mark owns a coffee shop and a customer, say, Harry, chooses to pay for dinner using Bitcoins. Mark has displayed his address or the QR code of his Bitcoin address at the top of the menu board in his shop for his customers to be able to pay with their Bitcoins. This is the public key of this wallet which is used for receiving the funds. Let's consider the cost for dinner to be 0.10 Bitcoin, also known as 100 millibits. To transfer the Bitcoins to Mark's account, if Harry is using the blockchain mobile wallet on an Android phone, he would see a screen requesting two inputs:

1. Receiver: The destination Bitcoin address for the transaction
2. Value: The amount of Bitcoin to send

Most of the crypto currency wallets provide a feature called send by QR code. Around the input field for the Bitcoin address, there is a small icon that looks like a QR code. This allows Harry to scan the barcode with his smartphone camera so that he doesn't have to type in Mark's Bitcoin address (e.g., 1Cdid9KFAaatwczBwBttQcwXYCpvK8h7FK), which is quite long and difficult to type. The mobile wallet application fills in the Bitcoin address scanning the QR code and Harry can check that it scanned correctly by comparing a few digits from the address with the address displayed by Mark. Harry then enters the Bitcoin value for the transaction, 0.10 Bitcoin. He then presses Send to transmit the transaction. Harry's mobile Bitcoin wallet constructs a transaction that assigns 0.10 Bitcoin to the address provided by Mark, sourcing the funds from Harry's wallet and signing the transaction with Harry's private keys. This tells the Bitcoin network that Harry has authorized a transfer of value from one of his addresses to Mark's new address. As the transaction is transferred via the peer-to-peer protocol, it quickly broadcasts across the Bitcoin network. In a split second, most of the nodes in the network receive the transaction and see Mark's address for the first time.

If Mark has a system with him, he will also be able to see the transaction online. The Bitcoin ledger is a constantly growing file that records every Bitcoin transaction that has ever occurred; it is public. That means that all Mark must

Fig. 7.9 Bitcoin transaction—real-world scenario

do is look up his own address in the blockchain network and see if any funds have been sent to it. He can do this quite easily at the blockchain.info website by entering his address in the search box. The website will show him a page listing all the transactions to and from that address. If Mark is watching that page, it will update to show a new transaction transferring 0.10 Bitcoin to his balance soon after Harry hits Send. Figure 7.9 illustrates this transaction.

At first, Mark's address will show the transaction from Harry as "Unconfirmed" since the transaction has been propagated to the network but has not yet been added in the Bitcoin transaction ledger (blockchain). To be included in the blockchain, the transaction must be picked up by a miner and included in a block of transactions. Once a new block is created—in the current situation it takes about ten minutes (Proof of Work and validation process)—the transactions within the block will be accepted as "confirmed" by the network and available to be spent. Now the transaction is seen by everyone immediately after it is included in a newly mined block. Mark is now the proud owner of 0.10 Bitcoin that he can spend. Mark can buy something using the Bitcoins he has now.

Types of Wallets

There are five different types of wallets available for digital currency that provide different ways to store and access your coins securely. Wallets can be classified into three distinct categories—software, hardware, and paper.

1. Desktop wallets are designed for PCs and Mac, which has to be downloaded and installed on the computer. Once installed, they are only accessible from the same computer in which they are installed. Desktop wallets are more secure; however, if your computer is hacked or infected by a virus then there is the possibility of you losing all your funds.
2. Online wallets are cloud-based software accessible from any computer from any location. They are very easy to access, but online wallets store your private keys in a centralized online storage and are managed by a third party, which makes them vulnerable to hacking attacks and theft.
3. Mobile wallets are software applications available on your favorite mobile app store for download and installation on your smartphones. These are the most convenient of all the wallets that can be used from anywhere including retail stores. Mobile wallets are simpler than desktop wallets due to resource limitations on the mobile, but they provide most of the essential features required for most of the transactions.
4. Hardware wallets store a user's private key in a hardware device such as USB. Hardware wallets provide options to make online transactions in a highly secured fashion by storing the user's private keys in an offline storage. Hardware wallets are compatible to be used over different protocols and support multiple crypto currencies. Users connect the wallet to their internet-enabled computer via the USB, enter their PIN or password to login to the wallet, and start making transactions. Hardware wallets come with a higher price point, but they are the best wallet for serious crypto currency holdings where spending a small sum toward securing the private keys is extremely critical to safeguard the value of the assets you own on the blockchain.
5. Paper wallets are a completely disconnected non-electronic way of storing the private keys. They are basically a physical copy of your public and private keys on paper. It is an old school traditional approach of maintaining your secret yourself. Transferring Bitcoin or any other type of crypto currency to your paper wallet is relatively straightforward and involves transfer of coins from an electronic wallet to the public address displayed on the printout of your paper wallet. To withdraw or send coins to another wallet, you will need to transfer funds from the paper wallet to a software wallet. This process is referred to as sweeping which can be done either manually entering your private keys or scanning a QR code that normally prints on the paper wallet.

Wallet Security

As we discussed in the earlier section, wallets are secure to varying degrees and subject to the type of wallet and the software provider. Online wallets are inherently riskier due to the centralized storage of the private keys, thereby exposing users to the vulnerabilities in the electronic platform which in rare cases can be exploited by hackers to steal your assets on a blockchain. On the other hand, hardware wallets are highly secure as they store user's private keys offline but come with a price tag and difficulty in accessing your keys for making the transactions. Although online wallets are prone to cyberattacks, it is highly advisable to take diligent security precautions when using any type of wallet.

> Always remember, losing your private keys is equivalent to losing your money. Whichever wallet you use, you must take extreme precautions and be very careful!

If your wallet gets hacked or you send money to an incorrect address or to a scammer, there is absolutely no way to recover lost currency or reverse the transaction. Let's now look at some precautions that will prevent you from great loss.

1. Backup the Keys—Backing up your wallet keys can save you a lot of turmoil and trouble. Anything can happen at any time; your phone might get lost or your computer might crash. Backing up your crypto currency wallets can come to your rescue and make a critical crypto-catastrophe into a minor problem that can be fixed without any loss of your crypto currency.
2. Cold Storage—Cold storage is achieved when crypto currency private keys are created and stored in a secure offline environment. Cold storage is important for anyone with high-value crypto holdings. Online computers are vulnerable to hackers and should not be used to store a significant amount of Bitcoins.
3. Hardware Wallet—These are the physical devices created to keep your crypto currency safe. When you request a payment, the hardware wallet's API creates and signs the transaction and provides a public key which is directed to the network by the API. This ensures that the signing keys never leave the hardware wallet. Hardware wallets come with support for advanced features such as multi-signature transactions.
4. Multi-Signature—Wallets are advanced security configuration available with most of the crypto currency platforms and supported by most of the popular wallets. It involves multiple stakeholders to be involved in a transaction. When you configure your Bitcoin address to be multi-signature then it requires another user(s) to sign the transaction along with you before the transaction can be broadcast to the blockchain network. The first multi-signature wallet was launched in the market by BitGo in 2013.

Appendix

Complete Token Contract for LUCKY DOG

```
pragma solidity ^0.4.16;

interface tokenRecipient { function receiveApproval(address _from, uint256 _value, address _token, bytes _extraData) external; }

contract LuckyCoin {
    // Public variables of the token
    string public name;
    string public symbol;
    uint8 public decimals = 18;
    // 18 decimals is the strongly suggested default, avoid changing it
    uint256 public totalSupply;

    // This creates an array with all balances
    mapping (address => uint256) public balanceOf;
    mapping (address => mapping (address => uint256)) public allowance;

    // This generates a public event on the blockchain that will notify clients
    event Transfer(address indexed from, address indexed to, uint256 value);

    // This notifies clients about the amount burnt
    event Burn(address indexed from, uint256 value);

    /**
     * Constructor function
     *
     * Initializes contract with initial supply tokens to the creator of the contract
     */
    function LuckyCoin (
        uint256 initialSupply,
        string tokenName,
        string tokenSymbol
    ) public {
        totalSupply = initialSupply * 10 ** uint256(decimals);  // Update total supply with the decimal amount
        balanceOf[msg.sender] = totalSupply;                // Give the creator all initial tokens
        name = tokenName;                                   // Set the name for display purposes
        symbol = tokenSymbol;                               // Set the symbol for display purposes
    }

    /**
     * Internal transfer, only can be called by this contract
     */
    function _transfer(address _from, address _to, uint _value) internal {
        // Prevent transfer to 0x0 address. Use burn() instead
        require(_to != 0x0);
        // Check if the sender has enough
        require(balanceOf[_from] >= _value);
        // Check for overflows
        require(balanceOf[_to] + _value >= balanceOf[_to]);
        // Save this for an assertion in the future
        uint previousBalances = balanceOf[_from] + balanceOf[_to];
        // Subtract from the sender
        balanceOf[_from] -= _value;
        // Add the same to the recipient
        balanceOf[_to] += _value;
        emit Transfer(_from, _to, _value);
        // Asserts are used to use static analysis to find bugs in your code. They should never fail
        assert(balanceOf[_from] + balanceOf[_to] == previousBalances);
    }

    /**
     * Transfer tokens
     *
     * Send `_value` tokens to `_to` from your account
     *
     * @param _to The address of the recipient
     * @param _value the amount to send
     */
    function transfer(address _to, uint256 _value) public {
        _transfer(msg.sender, _to, _value);
    }

    /**
     * Transfer tokens from other address
     *
     * Send `_value` tokens to `_to` on behalf of `_from`
     *
     * @param _from The address of the sender
     * @param _to The address of the recipient
     * @param _value the amount to send
     */
```

```
    function transferFrom(address _from, address _to, uint256 _value) public returns (bool success) {
        require(_value <= allowance[_from][msg.sender]);     // Check allowance
        allowance[_from][msg.sender] -= _value;
        _transfer(_from, _to, _value);
        return true;
    }

    /**
     * Set allowance for other address
     *
     * Allows `_spender` to spend no more than `_value` tokens on your behalf
     *
     * @param _spender The address authorized to spend
     * @param _value the max amount they can spend
     */
    function approve(address _spender, uint256 _value) public
        returns (bool success) {
        allowance[msg.sender][_spender] = _value;
        return true;
    }

    /**
     * Set allowance for other address and notify
     *
     * Allows `_spender` to spend no more than `_value` tokens on your behalf, and then ping the contract about it
     *
     * @param _spender The address authorized to spend
     * @param _value the max amount they can spend
     * @param _extraData some extra information to send to the approved contract
     */
    function approveAndCall(address _spender, uint256 _value, bytes _extraData)
        public
        returns (bool success) {
        tokenRecipient spender = tokenRecipient(_spender);
        if (approve(_spender, _value)) {
            spender.receiveApproval(msg.sender, _value, this, _extraData);
            return true;
        }
    }

    /**
     * Destroy tokens
     *
     * Remove `_value` tokens from the system irreversibly
     *
     * @param _value the amount of money to burn
     */
    function burn(uint256 _value) public returns (bool success) {
        require(balanceOf[msg.sender] >= _value);   // Check if the sender has enough
        balanceOf[msg.sender] -= _value;            // Subtract from the sender
        totalSupply -= _value;                      // Updates totalSupply
        emit Burn(msg.sender, _value);
        return true;
    }

    /**
     * Destroy tokens from other account
     *
     * Remove `_value` tokens from the system irreversibly on behalf of `_from`.
     *
     * @param _from the address of the sender
     * @param _value the amount of money to burn
     */
    function burnFrom(address _from, uint256 _value) public returns (bool success) {
        require(balanceOf[_from] >= _value);                // Check if the targeted balance is enough
        require(_value <= allowance[_from][msg.sender]);    // Check allowance
        balanceOf[_from] -= _value;                         // Subtract from the targeted balance
        allowance[_from][msg.sender] -= _value;             // Subtract from the sender's allowance
        totalSupply -= _value;                              // Update totalSupply
        emit Burn(_from, _value);
        return true;
    }
}
```

8

ICO Regulatory and Reporting Framework

Sarah Swammy, Richard Thompson, and Marvin Loh

There are great predictions on the potential of blockchain-based solutions to "revolutionize" everything from financial markets to the very way that we outright recognize human identity for billions of people around the globe. Initial solutions on blockchain were more centered around the financial industry, but the trend has shifted now to address a wide array of sectors, and the majority of them have a social impact. In the current world, technology is empowering society to research with new solutions and business models. Blockchain is a kind of technology that has the power to deal with significant inefficiencies and transform operations in the social sector and to improve our lifestyle. Blockchain's inherent characteristics of immutability, decentralization, and transparency help build trust across multiple systems. In this chapter, we will be demonstrating blockchain's capacity to create scalable social impact and to identify the elements that need to be reported to mitigate challenges in its application.

Let's consider a few real-life instances; blockchain applications could provide the means for establishing identities for individuals without ID cards, introducing finance and banking services for the underprovisioned class of populations and helping aid distributions to refugees with improved transparency and efficiency. Governments across the globe are taking measurements to put land registry information onto blockchains to improve transparency and evade third-party corruption and manipulation. Blockchain's countless potential applications for social impact range from increasing access to capital to tracking health and education data across multiple generations, to improving voter records and voting systems.

S. Swammy et al., *Crypto Uncovered*, https://doi.org/10.1007/978-3-030-00135-3_8

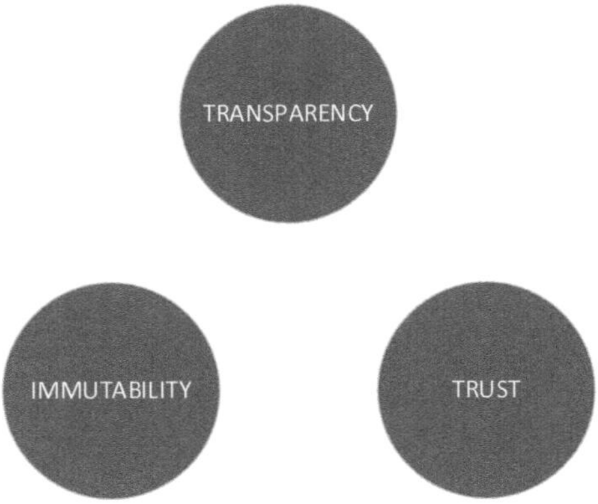

Fig. 8.1 Unique combinations of behavior

The social effects of blockchain can be powerful and lasting, while developers take on building these types of solutions. Blockchain has the potential to significantly impactful from the design, application, and approach to the development. With this kind of potential, the implementation of blockchain technologies has long-term implications for society and individuals. This chapter outlines why reporting is particularly crucial with blockchain and offers a framework to guide policymakers and social impact organizations to make appropriate design decisions to enable reporting right from the development of the solution. As social media, crypto currencies, and algorithms have shown, technology is not neutral. Values are embedded in the code. It is important to understand the manner in which the problem is defined and by whom, who is building the solution, the method in which it gets programmed and implemented, who has access, and what rules are created have consequences in intentional and unintentional ways. In the applications and implementation of blockchain, it is critical to understand that seemingly innocuous design choices have resounding ethical implications on people's lives. It is essential to ensure that proper provisions are made in the system for the required level of reporting.

Design Considerations for Reporting

Once blockchain comes out as appropriate technology, it is important to analyze the following areas of interest to ensure there is enough reporting coverage in the system. At each stage, guiding questions identify the effects of the design choices on the end users and communities.

1. Governance—How is **governance** created and maintained?
2. Identity—How is **identity** defined and established?
3. Verification and Authentication—How are inputs **verified** and transactions **authenticated**?
4. Access Control—How is **access** defined, granted, and executed?
5. Data Ownership—How is **the ownership** of data defined, granted, and executed?
6. Security—The manner in which **security** is set up and ensured.

Governance

Governance refers to the establishment and maintenance of the rules that govern the entire blockchain system. A fundamental characteristic of blockchain technology is having a rigid set of rules by which all transactions within the system are governed. In the social sector, it is critical to ensure that a sound human governance structure is driving the technology. Governance includes questions such as who sets up the rules, who maintains the system, how the rules are executed, and how a blockchain system would be closed out. The established governance structure should also be responsible for ensuring adherence to the guiding principles and design philosophy of the project.

Following are the key design considerations for reporting on Governance:

- Determining who the stakeholders are, their roles, and how their roles are established.
- Establishing the processes, rules, and regulations of governance (both technical and otherwise).
- Creating pathways for these rules and roles to change over time.
- Having a plan for closing out or continuing the system if key stakeholders leave.

Identity

Significant ethical considerations surround what constitutes "identity" and to whom identity is granted in a given blockchain, and the manner in which identity information is used, accessed, and protected. Multiple pieces of identifying information collectively create a digital identity. Blockchains can be used to establish limited, or transactional, digital identities for accessing information or services. Portable, foundational digital identities can also be established using blockchain systems. Portable, foundational digital identities are the identities that are permanently linked to a unique individual and hence can be used in a variety of contexts, moving with the individual, to prove identity or credentials.

Following are the key design considerations for reporting on Identity:

- Understand who is granted identity in this context.
- Understand the solution identity level.
  - *Note:* a transactional identity can be considered as a limited-purpose identity. It grants a person single-use or limited access to a certain service. On the other hand, a foundational identity serves as a fully functioning identity that can be used for many purposes over time.
- Determine the identifiers that will be used to constitute this entity.
- Prevent exposure of personally identifiable information on a blockchain.
  - This may require never putting personally identifiable information directly on a blockchain.

Verification and Authentication

Verification of inputs and then its authentication is important in an open ledger system. The process of verifying information put onto a blockchain comes with a lot of challenges. The verification process for digital assets like crypto currencies or digital photographs is closely related to the transaction authentication process. It is done to determine if the entity that initiated a transaction has any control over that asset. When a non-digital asset, such as a person or an object, is linked to a blockchain, complication increases in verification because it introduces human interaction and, therefore, various political, legal, and ethical obstacles. For instance, how can someone's claim of land ownership be verified?

Following are the key design considerations for reporting on Verification and Authentication:

- Determining how and by whom verification will be done for the initial entry, or "zero state," follow-on data input, and how transactions between users are authenticated.
  - This includes setting up both information vetting processes and technical structures that prevent invalid entries.
- Ensuring that all stakeholders can trust the established process.
- Understand any economic, legal, political, and social impact of consensus protocol algorithms.

Access Control

Access definition, granting, and execution are critical for any person for using and interacting with a blockchain system. Also, the scope of access to individuals' personal information on a blockchain may result in serious implications for those individuals if that information is exploited. Beyond the specifics of accessing a blockchain to view or write to the ledger, access also includes more intangible questions around digital literacy and the effective ability to access the system.

Following are the key design considerations for reporting on Access Control:

- Who has permissions to write?
- Who has permissions to read?
- The manner in which the permissions are established.
- The level of access that users are given.

Data Ownership

There are some important questions like the owner of the data, who exercises control over the data, where and the manner in which the data is stored, and how adjustments are made to incorrect information. A fascinating characteristic of blockchain is its ability to give users the power to exercise functional control over data. It has the potential to answer questions on the owner of the data, exercising control over the data, where and the manner in which the data is stored, and how incorrect information is adjusted. For example, the Sovrin Foundation is building a self-sovereign identity trust framework that creates a robust governance structure that allows people to exert positive control over their personal digital identity information.

Following are the key design considerations for reporting on Data Ownership:

- Understanding who owns data, both in name and in practice.
- Knowing and understanding the manner in which stakeholders will be able to use the owned data and thus benefit from it.
- Deciding if data will be stored externally or in the blockchain.
  - Considering data storage options that are decentralized.
- Creating a process for users where they will be able to flag and fix incorrect information.

Security

A distributed infrastructure can have data scattered all over it. This, in turn, reduces the vulnerabilities compared with data that is aggregated and stored in one location. It is not necessary for users to remember passwords. In fact, it is also not necessary for them to link their personal information, like emails or contact numbers, to collections of stored information. However, there are ethical challenges here as well. Blockchain security uses encryption algorithms and the use of public/private key pairs that are like a publicly known "address" and a private digital key to essentially unlock the mailbox at that address. Blockchain technologies have been increasingly used for securing private information like health records. At an individual level, this refers to a user's understanding of potential risks as well as private key management. At the system level, this refers to potential vulnerabilities within and at the periphery of the system. What would happen in case of loss of digital key that is used to control assets or medical information?

Following are the key design considerations for reporting on Data Ownership:

- Determining who establishes security as well as who is responsible for breaching it.
- To ensure that vulnerable data is adequately protected against current and future threats.
- Deciding the manner in which different pieces of information will be protected.
- Creating a system for safe and effective access to private keys.

Blockchain Ecosystem

Any solution on blockchain is driven by an ecosystem comprised of these factors: the user, community, existing infrastructure, and financials. Therefore, it is very important from a reporting perspective to conduct a ecosystem assessment. This assessment will help to understand and acknowledge the roles that each of these core components plays in contributing to the blockchain-based solution. The roles of these components are mostly connected via a web of complex interactions. These roles may vary throughout the project timeline. However, ecosystems are not static, they are fluid and thus continue to change and evolve throughout the entire life cycle of the project. It is important to understand not only natural changes to the ecosystem but also the manner in which the implementation and the design of a blockchain solution may affect (hasten or spur) these processes. The assessment should also be periodically revisited to inform and evaluate key design choices. It should also be updated and reconsidered as the project progresses.

Users

At the outset of the ecosystem assessment, the end users of a blockchain tool must be identified, and thus the ecosystem has to be understood from the end users' perspective. Understanding this end-user perspective involves in-depth research and conversations. It also involves an inclusive design process to fully understand the identity of the end users, their needs, their vulnerabilities, and any other risks they might be facing. All these needs, vulnerabilities, and risks in the present state as well as their potential evolution in possible future contexts have to be evaluated.

User Assessment Questions

- Who are the users?
  - Important key attributes of the users.

    Digital literacy of users.
    Context literacy of users.
  - The reason behind these being the end users of the desired outcome.
- Needs/goals of the users.
  - The manner in which these might change over time.
- Vulnerabilities of the users.
  - The manner in which these might change over time.
- Risks to the users.
  - The manner in which these might change over time.

Community

In addition to identifying the end users of the blockchain, their identity and community also need to be understood. This includes understanding the borders of the community, or communities. The dynamics within and between them also needs to be understood. When a community is considered, it is crucial to pay attention to what dynamics and systemic forces are at play, as well as the roles and relationships of all of the community members irrespective of their being direct blockchain end users. Developing this kind of understanding requires cooperation from community members to identify, for example, who could provide a good or service that is integral to the desired outcome, who could provide the identity necessary to access that good or service, and who in the community could authenticate the validity of the identity claims.

Community Assessment Questions

- The relevant boundaries of the community that includes physical, social, cultural, and economic.
  - Possibility of these boundaries conflicting with one another.
- Relationships that are important in the community.
  - Nominal power holder in the community.
  - Effective power holder in the community.
  - The manner in which the distribution of power is established.
  - Possibility of having marginalized or vulnerable community members.

    The possibility of having internal threats to certain members of the community.
  - Are these relationships formalized or informal?
- Relationship of the community with external actors.
  - The various external organizations that have relationships within the community.

    The relationship with all community members or a particular subset.
  - Possibility of any external threats to members of the community.

- Community-level needs/goals.
  - The change it might bring in the future.
- What are community-level vulnerabilities?
  - How might these change in the future?
- What are community-level risks?
  - How might these change in the future? (Consider the evolution of technology, climate change, changes in power.)

Infrastructure

It is crucial to understand the infrastructure that binds members of the community together for achieving a new desired outcome. Legal and regulatory frameworks, public policies, informal rules or systems, and data and other assets could be part of this infrastructure. Leveraging these structures can be done to achieve the desired outcome. It may also create friction or barriers during the implementation of blockchain tools. The potential to create friction for these structures could occur at any stage of the project—from design to development, to deployment, to implementation, to sustainment, to the potential termination or transition of blockchain tools.

Infrastructure Assessment Questions

- The manner in which the current infrastructure reaches the outcome.
  - Where in the process is improvement occurring (time saving, cost saving)?

    The possibility of this improvement being replicated by a completely new blockchain system.

    If not, the manner in which the opportunity costs of remaining with the old system are balanced.
- The policies, legal and regulatory frameworks, informal systems, cultural and social systems, and other processes that are in place which might affect the desired outcome.
  - The elements of the infrastructure that could be leveraged in the blockchain solution.
  - Factors or dynamics that may disrupt or prevent the execution of the solution.

- Current existing data.
  - Ownership of the data.
  - Accuracy of the data.

    Is there a universal or adequate acceptance of its accuracy?

  - Preciseness of the data.
  - Comprehensively of the data.
  - The manner in which it is stored.

Financials

The implementation of a blockchain tool is driven by financial incentives that influence every stage of the project life cycle. Thus, it is important to understand the manner in which a blockchain would be financed, and who would benefit financially from its implementation. Understanding who would be hurt financially from its implementation and how financial hurdles might alter key design choices are also important.

Financial Assessment Questions

- Financial incentives of the entity building a blockchain.
- The manner in which the blockchain would be financed at each stage in the process.
- Financially who would benefit from the implementation of a blockchain and how?
- Financial incentives that are needed for keeping the current system in place.
  - Who would be harmed financially from the implementation of a new blockchain?
- Sustainability of the funding model for the blockchain.
- Are there financial hurdles that would drive design decisions?
  - Would the resulting design decisions increase or decrease user utility?
  - Would the resulting design decisions increase or decrease user risk?

Reporting

As centralized initiatives are diligently launched to implement a regulation framework around digital currencies in general, it is imperative that entrepreneurs who are in this space be proactive and forward-thinking and implement a reporting framework for any portal that a client faces in a crypto currency enterprise. Oftentimes reporting frameworks are included into the original designs of platforms and are more than often backfilled or outsourced to third-party software. It is more prudent to take no chances because of the highly regulatory nature of the security industry to make implementing a reporting framework a high priority. One of the many benefits of taking the approach of architecting the portal around a governance framework is that a reporting framework is intuitively design. Referring to Chap. 4 based upon a governance framework that incorporates participant management adhering to roles, activities, events entitlements, a natural reporting framework can be constructed. Based upon the governance framework a general parameterized reporting platform becomes a natural fit.

As participants are onboarded within the network through a registration process a unique encrypted ID is assigned to each individual or entity that desires to become a member of the network. General information from that participant is collected during this process along with supporting documents to satisfy the KYC regulations. All information goes through a verification process to certify all information accepting all applicants who pass the validation process and rejecting others. The KYC process is necessary, although it may appear to violate the privacy and anonymity principles of crypto currencies. Separating the architecture design of the marketplace that defines the context and transaction nature of the currency from the underlying payments system that facilitates decentralized transactions components allows the harmony of the crypto enterprise to exist. Crypto currency without a defined marketplace based upon historical analysis would be a game played among a niche group of software and technology enthusiasts. Reaching a critical mass without a marketplace would be nearly impossible.

The marketplace is the value-added surface that brings relevance to digital currency. A compromise is reached to keep the entrepreneurs, who are brave enough to champion innovation in digital currency, from suffering the threat of serious legal ramifications and having a viable business. As demonstrated, the governance framework has a natural reporting structure as participants are recorded using a private highly secured network, a VPN, as discussed previously in Chap. 4.

The data model constructed will include unique ID and location details of individuals. Additional information important to the reporting process, such as initial registration date, process date, and member date, need to be recorded. Implementing this concept at a minimal, using these three types of dates reports, actual dates that participants registered will provide a mechanism to report on how efficient the marketplace is. The time difference between an initial registration and when the registration was officially acknowledged and began to become processed will give an indication of the efficiency of the administration and registration process of the marketplace. The time difference between the initial registration date and the member date minus the lag from the process date would give an indication about the efficiency of the individual providing the verification documentation needed to satisfy registration requirements. These subtitle parameters provide an insight into managing efficiency to the owners of the portal. If the verification process is taking longer than average, they also provide a warning to owners that individuals may be providing fraudulent information to get verified documents in place.

It is best for owners to have as much insight as possible since they are the one facing a legal risk, as members come online and their account becomes active and able to hold currency. The governance framework comprising events and actions will record member account activity and maintain current position holdings. These details begin to shape some standardized reports that must be instituted within any financial account management which are personal account summary. Before laying out the personal account summary, let's analyze the general structure of the reporting framework. The portal will allow reporting experiences based upon the login roles. If the individual is a site administrator they would have different reporting entitlements than that of an individual user. An individual user may also have different reporting features. To satisfy the minimum requirements for compliance, it is sufficient to focus on administrating duty of reporting roles, members assigned to roles, rules on activity levels that go over rule thresholds. In addition to site administrators providing regulatory reporting to governing agents, facilities to individual members is a requirement also.

Having the underlying infrastructure to create indexes and tagged data elements from a defined data model makes parametrized reporting possible. As a best practice, designing the reporting foundation implementing the Application Programming Interface is most essential to create a feature-rich user reporting experience. To provide a minimum reporting set to satisfy regulators using the natural generalized framework start by indexing out roles. Each role category will have a unique ID, which could be a system numeric ID. Ensure the model contains an alpha identifier up to a certain specified length and contains a description element that provides further clarity.

As roles are created, the reporting function can provide a viewable list as to the dichotomy of the participants. Referring to Chap. 4 architecting the LUCKY DOG world, the following roles would be created:

Id: ldr0001
roleCode: ADM
name: Administrator
description: Site administrator and entitlement officer

Id: ldr0002
roleCode:VNDR
name: Vendor
description: Business service proprietor

Additional roles are created in this manner for possibly owner, authenticator, economic participant. Id, rolecode, and name are elements that are possibly indexed out to provide a parametrized search for roles. Other data entities created as part of the architecture are users, action types, acctActivity. Creating at a minimum, the specified design, reports able to be generated that list user users of a specified role.

Listing the follow reports would satisfy reporting requirements:

Parameterized reporting involves having the ability to index out data elements within the framework to run queries and return a result set. Following these guidelines entrepreneurs can extend the base setup and develop fully enriched services.

Table 8.1 view_all_roles

Roles		
RoleCode	**Name**	**Description**
ADM	Administrator	Site Administrator and Entitlement Officer
VND	Vendor	Service Proprietor
AUTH	Authenticator	Validator of Pure Canine Breed
BRDR	Breeder	Canine Breedor
OWN	Owner	Owner of Pure Breed Canine

Table 8.2 view_all_rolesByID

Roles VND		
RoleCode	**Name**	**Description**
VND	Vendor	Service Proprietor

Table 8.3 view_all_users

Users						
Name		Address				
First	**Last**	**Country**	**Provence**	**City**	**email**	**Role**
Tom	Brown	USA	Ca	San Jose	tbrown@lcy.com	ADM
Susan	Jones	USA	Wi	Madison	sbrown@lcy.com	OWN
Maria	Gomez	MEX	CDMX	Mexico City	mgomez@lcy.com	AUTH
Luis	Rodriguez	BRZ	Sao Paulo	Osaco	lrodriguex@lcy.com	BRD

Table 8.4 view_all_usersByID

Users sbrown@lcy						
Name		Address				
First	**Last**	**Country**	**Provence**	**City**	**email**	**Role**
Susan	Jones	USA	Wi	Madison	sbrown@lcy.com	OWN

Table 8.5 view_all_userByRole

Role	AUTH					
Name		Address				
First	**Last**	**Country**	**Provence**	**City**	**email**	**Role**
Maria	Gomez	MEX	CDMX	Mexico City	mgomez@lcy.com	AUTH

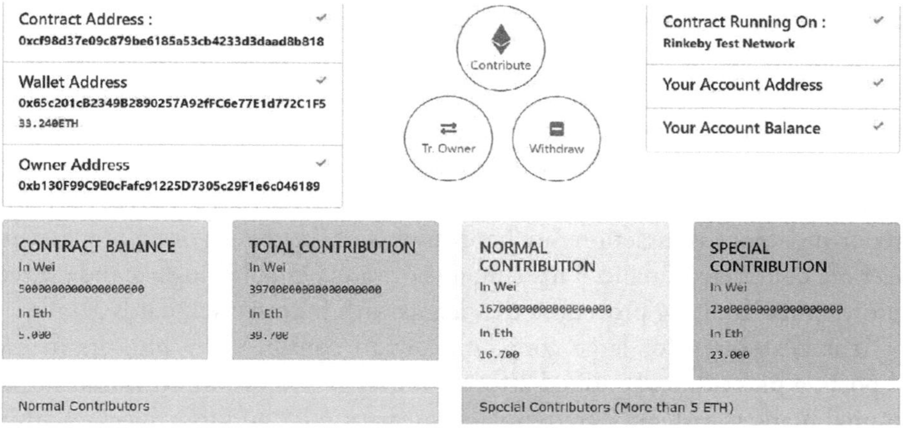

Fig. 8.2 Account summary

Apart from profile report and activity reporting, it is essential to have an account summary showing coin holding and current market value.

Dimensions

A more complex type of reporting and analysis involves a platform exposing dimension. In our data model, three dates were added to the user record: regDate, procDate, memDate. Having categories, specialized dates allow for dimensional analysis to take place. A time series can be created by user account balances over a given time period. Also, reports require creating categories that have the ability to index on those categories.

Analytics

As more and more data is being produced and collected, it is a natural use case for big data analysis. In our LUCKY DOG marketplace, the blockchain will record the transaction of canine breeds, the selling price set by particular breeders, grooming services, authentication prices. The blockchain can be interrogated by artificial intelligence processes that are able to create sets of data. These sets of data are sampled at different sets of time and fed into a machine-learning engine. As these neuronetworks grow these data sets can produce ranking in breeds of dogs, rankings on breeders, vendors, and many more as data sets are created. Service recommendation lists are possible to be created by the sets as specific users' activity is interrogated through the blockchain.

Financial Reporting and Auditing

The LUCKY DOG marketplace has the building blocks to create reports to manage users, record daily activity, and compute theoretical values of individual holdings. However, to stay in business and steer clear of any suspicion of being a rogue marketplace, the owner should institute a formal auditing reporting. Since transactions are happening and the tokens or crypto currencies are considered financial instruments of value, establishing a standardized professional auditing procedure that aligns with industry standards is safe.

It is customary for large conglomerates to consult CPA auditors in the reporting procedure of audited information as they help a multitrillion-dollar capital markets system operation with integrity. CPA auditors operate within tight regulations and maintain extremely high auditing standards and professional codes of conduct. These CPA entities are always independent to ensure unbiased reporting. CPA auditing professionals follow detailed objective-driven procedures and exercise professional skepticism to ensure that a corporate financial statements does not contain material misstatements. And in certain instances they determine if internal financial reporting controls are effective. The role of professional CPA in the auditing process is necessary and vital to the integrity of many industries. However, blockchain technology brings the virtue of immutable record keeping, which raises an important discussion point whether this powerful technology may drastically reduce or eliminate the need for a financial statement audited by a CPA.

Examining the process further reveals that there are limits to blockchain in respect to reporting. However, having a proactive framework in place at conception is the regulatory responsibility for any entrepreneur having a crypto market. As our LUCKY DOG market example demonstrates, the blockchain can accurately and reliably provide a verifiable transaction between a breeder and a buyer. However, the blockchain cannot report whether a dog that was delivered is in good health or free from any physical defects.

Hence, blockchain records may not always provide sufficient audit evidence relating to the nature of the transaction. A transaction recorded in a blockchain may still be as follows:

- classified incorrectly
- executed between non-independent parties
- unauthorized, fraudulent, or illegal
- linked to a side agreement that is "off-chain."

Furthermore, estimated values can leak into transactions recorded on the blockchain. A reconciliation between historical values and estimated values must occur. In such events, independent auditors are mandatory.

With the increased adoption of blockchain, central locations may become equipped to obtain audit data. These centralized enriched data become invaluable resources for auditors, making it wise to develop standard procedures to obtain audit information directly from the blockchain. Proper cleansing controls are necessary to ensure confidence that the data is reliable. As data flows to the public blockchain, it must be carefully determined if the cleansing procedures, workflow, or protocols can be manipulated or compromised under certain conditions. These precautionary assessments are necessary since many of the entities will not have control over the auditing data.

Using blockchain for formal financial reporting in the audit process may be corporate initiatives which will require an update and reevaluation of management accounting policies for digital assets and liabilities. Currently, these policies have not been directly addressed in international financial reporting procedures or domestic accounting principles. The professional auditing communities must refit the audit procedures to take advantage of the virtues of blockchain as well as address the inherent risk.

The opportunity to streamline financial reporting is more appealing for many institutions versus the effort of overcoming the reporting complexities associated with the blockchain, given that myriad files containing data for reconciliation, account information, journal entries, extracts, subledgers, supporting spreadsheets, and trial balances are delivered to CPA auditors in a variety of digital and manual formats. Streamlining this process is significant. The chance for CPA auditors to have near real-time data access from read-only nodes on the blockchain is invaluable and provides a significant cost benefit of time and financial savings.

As more and more entities and processes migrate to blockchain solutions, accessing information in the blockchain will likely become more efficient. For example, if a significant class of transactions for an industry is recorded in a blockchain, it might be possible for a CPA auditor to develop software to continuously audit organizations using the blockchain. This could eliminate many of the manual data extraction and audit preparation activities that are labor-intensive and time-consuming for an entity's management and staff. Speeding up audit preparation activities could help reduce the lag between the transaction and verification dates—one of the major criticisms of financial reporting. Reducing lag time could offer the opportunity to increase the efficiency and effectiveness of financial reporting and auditing by enabling management and auditors to focus on riskier and more complex transactions while conducting routine auditing in near real time. With blockchain-enabled digitization, auditors could deploy more automation, analytics, and machine-learning capabilities such as automatically alerting relevant parties about unusual transactions on a near real-time basis. Supporting documentation, such as contracts, agreements, purchase orders, and invoices, could be encrypted and securely stored or linked to a blockchain. By giving CPA auditors access to unalterable audit evidence, the pace of financial reporting and auditing could be improved. While the audit process may become more continuous, auditors will still have to apply professional judgment when analyzing accounting estimates and other judgments made by management in the preparation of financial statements. In addition, for areas that become automated, they will also need to evaluate and test internal controls over the data integrity of all sources of relevant financial information.

As blockchain systems standardize transaction processing across many industries, a CPA, including CPA auditors, may be able to provide assurance to users of the technology. The CPA may be able to fill a potential future role because of their skill sets, independence, objectivity, and expertise. The following list of potential new roles for a CPA is illustrative only and not all-inclusive; significant regulatory and professional hurdles may remain before a CPA is able to take on these potential roles.

Auditor of Smart Contracts and Oracles

As described above, smart contracts can be embedded in a blockchain to automate business processes. Contracting parties may want to engage an assurance provider to verify that smart contracts are implemented with the correct business logic. In addition, a CPA auditor could verify the interface between smart contracts and external data sources that trigger business events. Without an independent evaluation, users of blockchain technologies face the risk of unidentified errors or vulnerabilities. CPA auditors may have to expand their skill set, including understanding technical programming language and the functions of a blockchain, to adopt these challenging roles. This type of role also raises important questions for the auditing profession, including:

- How to redefine skill sets for certain professions to remain relevant?
- What factors would impact assurance engagement risk?
- What would an assurance provider's ongoing responsibility entail once a smart contract is released into a blockchain?

In the scope of a financial statement audit, management will be responsible for establishing controls to verify whether the smart contract source code is consistent with the intended business logic. An independent CPA auditing an entity with smart contracts/blockchain is likely to consider management's controls over the smart contract code. However, many companies may choose to reuse smart contracts built by other entities already active on a blockchain. Future auditing standards and auditing guidance may need to contemplate this technology and thereby bring clarity to the role of the CPA auditor in those scenarios.

Service Auditor of Consortium Blockchains

Prior to launching a new application on an existing blockchain platform or leveraging or subscribing to an existing blockchain product, users of the system may desire independent assurance as to the stability and robustness of its architecture. Instead of each participant performing their own due diligence, it may be more efficient to hire a CPA to achieve these objectives. In addition, critical blockchain elements (e.g., cryptographic key management) should be designed to include sophisticated GITCs that provide ongoing protection for sensitive information, as well as processing controls over security, availability, processing integrity, privacy, and confidentiality. On an ongoing basis, a trusted and independent third party may be needed to provide a quantitative assessment as to the effectiveness of controls over a private blockchain. This type of service raises important questions for the profession:

- When providing assurance across a blockchain, who is the client?
- How would a CPA auditor assess engagement risk for an autonomous system?
- How would independence rules apply to users of a blockchain?

Administrator Function

Industry-accepted blockchain solutions may be proven beneficial from a known, unbiased independent third party to administrate a central access-granting function. This role could be responsible for identity verification or for conducting a vetting process to be completed by a participant before they are granted access to a blockchain. This central administrator could validate the enforcement and monitoring of the blockchain's protocols. A possible undue advantage could be given to a single user/node of the blockchain if it performed the administration function. This particular orientation would compromise trust among consortium members. Strict attention is necessary when establishing the role and legal responsibility of the administrator because this function administrates the entire blockchain. As a trusted professional, an independent CPA may be capable of carrying out this responsibility. However, this role would raise new questions for the profession:

- By taking on such a critical role, is the assurance provider independent from the blockchain participants?
- Could the CPA auditor conduct financial statement audits on those participants?

Arbitration Function

Business arrangements can be complex and may result in disputes between even the most well-intentioned parties. For a permissioned blockchain, an arbitration function might be needed in the future to settle disputes among the consortium-blockchain participants. This function is analogous to the executor of an estate, a role typically filled by various qualified professionals, including CPA auditors. Participants on the blockchain may require this type of function to enforce contract terms where the spirit of the smart contract departs from a legal document, contractual agreement, or letter. Further considerations should be explored to determine whether an arbitration function is necessary. If CPAs want to take on this role, the following critical questions will need to be answered:

- What legal framework would be used to settle disputes?
- What skill set would be required for a CPA auditor?
- Could this role create unintended threats to independence regarding attest clients?

The implementation and adoption of blockchain in the auditing function is evolving very rapidly. And the complete scope of how the technology will impact the industry overall is not clear as many unknowns still exist. Blockchain is penetrating the industry as CPA auditors are starting to use blockchain transactions in organization auditing process. The rate of adoption will increase but blockchain technology will not replace financial reporting and financial auditing statements in the immediate future. A marketplace providing a clear auditing function will limit any suspicion of a rogue business operation.

9

Crypto Currency: Another Block in the Continuum of Value Exchange

Dan Castro

The other chapters of this book discuss the details and inner workings of crypto currencies. This short chapter simply takes a look at the opportunity and the risk inherent in adopting a new way of exchanging value or transacting trade. This chapter is also going to dispense with the hyperbole surrounding crypto currency—there will be no discussion of revolutionary technology, new economic paradigms, or disrupting history; rather, this chapter simply wants to look at this new medium of exchange and how it may or may not do anything more than provide another alternative to people for the buying and selling of goods and services.

Historical Backdrop

Crypto currency is simply the latest method for people to buy and sell goods and services. Before there were any currencies, people bartered between themselves either exchanging things of value between themselves or exchanging services for things of value. As time progressed, certain items of value, such as precious metals (gold, silver) or commodities (grains, livestock) were used as a medium of exchange. In the next iteration of exchange, coins of various size, shapes, and materials were utilized as money, and most coins had intrinsic value based on the materials they were composed of. Eventually paper currency became the standard of exchange. At various times, paper currency has been backed by land, precious metals, or other items of value. In the twentieth century until the Great Depression, most of the industrialized nations of the world used the Gold Standard to back their currencies, where the value of

S. Swammy et al., *Crypto Uncovered*, https://doi.org/10.1007/978-3-030-00135-3_9

their currencies was related to the value of the gold they held in storage to back those currencies. After WWII the "gold exchange standard" was established by the Bretton Woods Agreement, setting the official exchange rate at $35 per ounce of gold. In 1971, the US moved off of the gold exchange standard, allowing supply and demand to determine the value of its currency. Since then, the relative value of currencies has been backed not by one particular asset, but by governments' creditworthiness and the faith of the public in their ability to pay back any debts owed by them. The abandonment of the gold standard helped alleviate the need for governments to stockpile large supplies of gold, but it also forced countries to seek new means to guarantee stability for their currencies as they "floated" freely against one another.

Over the past few decades, new financial instruments such as options, swaps, and futures have allowed currencies to be exchanged in new ways. For consumers, the introduction of credit cards, debit cards, and other means of transferring money (wire transfers) has increased the velocity and volume of currency or money transfer. In the modern era, currency has evolved from being physical to being digital as well. Now, unlike sovereign currencies, crypto currencies do not have physical form on paper; they are digital and are exchanged or traded in electronic digital environments.

Crypto Currency Wallet Security

At their heart, crypto currencies currently reside on a vast network of peer-to-peer computers with an immutable, distributed database called the blockchain. This is all well described in other chapters. While the cryptography of the network appears secure, the means of accessing the network—crypto currency wallets—may not be any more secure than credit cards. A crypto currency wallet is a software application that stores the public and private keys that interface with the blockchain. If your crypto currency wallet is compromised you could lose your crypto currency. Some crypto currency wallets are desktop wallets designed for use on PCs. If your computer is hacked your crypto currency is at risk. Some crypto currency wallets are cloud-based and accessible from computers anywhere, but clouds like credit cards are managed by a third party, so hacking and theft are a possibility just like they are with any database controlled by a third party. Mobile wallets designed for smartphones are convenient, but smartphones can be hacked, lost, or stolen. There are also hardware wallets housed in devices such as USBs which are highly secure, unless the USB is lost, stolen, or damaged. Lastly, there are paper crypto currency wallets that are essentially paper copies of your public and private keys, so they are no more secure than paper currency.

Given the above, crypto currency wallets do not appear to provide any more security, depending on the form of the wallet, than other data you store on your computer, in the cloud, on your smart phone, or in your own personal physical wallet. So, while the blockchain itself may be secure and immutable as a distributed ledger, the means of accessing the blockchain, the crypto currency wallet, is no more secure than other methods of exchanging goods and services. If your private key is lost or compromised, your crypto currency is at risk.

The Next Block in the Chain

At present, crypto currencies will not replace sovereign currencies as the primary medium for exchange of goods and services. However, crypto currencies are a viable complement as an alternative medium of exchange for anyone with access to a computer or smartphone. Perhaps the biggest challenge is acceptance and use by both consumers and sellers of goods and services. Multiple sovereign governments are building and/or improving the legal frameworks and infrastructure for the growth, development, and safety of crypto currencies. In similar fashion to security regulation, government regulators will need to ensure that money laundering, fraud, and predatory or criminal activities are controlled or eliminated. Simultaneously, vendors or sellers of goods and services will need to accept crypto currencies and be protected in the same way as they are when consumers use credit cards. At present, a credit card transaction takes a few seconds to be approved and executed; the typical Bitcoin transaction takes roughly ten minutes for the blockchain to be validated. This may be a significant issue if crypto currencies are to be widely accepted and used by the general public. This is not unexpected; it is simply another step in the evolution of the blockchain, and of how we transact business.

10

A Vision for the Future: The Bermuda FinTech Story

E. David Burt, Sarah Swammy, Richard Thompson, and Marvin Loh

In order to advance the types of innovations we have discussed throughout the book, it will require the commitment and collaboration of governments, technology firms, and academic institutions. This collaboration could lead to sustainable economic growth and the betterment of our overall society.

We are at a pivotal point in our history where through advances in technology we have been given both the gift and the responsibility of massive amounts of data and the tools to interpret and create new frontiers in many fields. Crypto currency is one of the most talked about advances. Technology has enabled access to create and trade digital currency and put the opportunity to participate into the hands of the public in a decentralized and not fully regulated manner.

At its core, government has the responsibility to protect its citizens, to provide parameters for behavior, and to provide for their well-being. In that vein, it is government that records and stores the recordation life's most basic and fundamental events and occurrences.

When a child is born, it is government that provides the birth certificate. When that same child becomes an adult and purchase a home, purchase a car, votes in elections, and possibly gets married, it is government that records and stores that data. Finally, when that same person passes away, it is government that issues a death certificate.

S. Swammy et al., *Crypto Uncovered*, https://doi.org/10.1007/978-3-030-00135-3_10

Blockchain Potential

Since the role of recording and storing information and data is fundamental for the government, they have the unwavering duty to have a system that is built upon trust. Citizens must trust that their information and data is secure with the government. Our citizens' most basic information and data must be secure from hacks and breaches from within our borders and outside our state and country.

The nature and technology of blockchain seems very promising in a world where government must provide a safe haven for storing and transferring records. The distributed nature and trust verification process of blockchain is potentially of great use to our government and must be fast-tracked and implemented expeditiously. The deployment of these core technologies can lead to a more transparent and efficient government and benefit society.

The application of these concepts is demonstrated in the working example "The Bermuda FinTech Story: Building on a reputation for innovation and collaboration" by the Premier of Bermuda, the Hon. E. David Burt, JP, MP.

The Bermuda FinTech Story: Building on a Reputation for Innovation and Collaboration

A Brief History of Bermuda

Where is Bermuda? The earliest known map to have Bermuda depicted dates back to 1505. The island, located in the North Atlantic Ocean, was discovered by Spanish explorer Juan de Bermudez, after whom the island is named.

It wasn't until 1609 that settlers, on their way from England to Jamestown, Virginia, were shipwrecked, during what is believed to be a hurricane, and came ashore. Bermuda is credited for saving the lives of settlers in Jamestown, Virginia; those who survived the Bermuda storm rebuilt their boats and carried wild hogs, fish, birds and eggs, all of which were found in abundance on the island. The settlers who landed in Bermuda were able to feed their fellow settlers who by all historical accounts were starving to death.

From 1612 onward, the tiny island some 21 miles long and 1 mile at its widest point was claimed and settled by the British.

Over the next 400 years, Bermuda evolved into a modern society:

1616—The Bermuda Court of General Assize was established
1858—The first bank was established
1904—Electricity was introduced
1946—Cars were generally used and the first broadcasting company was established
1968—Bermuda's Constitutional Order came into effect and the first general election was held under universal adult suffrage

Bermuda is a self-governing British Overseas Territory.

The Economy

During the seventeenth century, the economy of Bermuda was whaling, shipbuilding, growing tobacco, and the start of the salt-raking trade with the Turks and Caicos Islands.

Between the 1600s and the 1800s, the economy was fueled by slavery which wasn't abolished in Bermuda until 1834. The 1700s also saw Bermuda become a privateering economy as a result of hostilities between England and Europe.

During the 1800s, exporting vegetables, especially Bermuda onions, in the spring to the eastern US became the mainstay of the economy together with the growing and shipping of Bermuda Easter lilies (*Lilium longiflorum*) and bulbs.

With mild temperatures, stunning beauty, and less than 700 miles from the US, in the late 1800s and early 1900s, Bermuda emerged as a popular vacation destination among wealthy Americans. Author and humorist Mark Twain famously stated, "You can go to heaven if you want to. I'd rather stay in Bermuda." Tourism was the mainstay of Bermuda's economy until the 1980s when it was slowly replaced by international business which began to move forward as a viable economic option for the island.

Today, Bermuda's international business portfolio includes insurance and reinsurance, captive insurance, life and annuity insurance, insurance-linked securities, asset management, trusts and private client vehicles, family offices, shipping and aviation registries, shipping finance and ship management, arbitration, filming and technology, and life sciences.

Over the years Bermuda has developed a reputation for innovation and collaboration in insurance and reinsurance. Industry professionals together with the government and the Bermuda Monetary Authority work closely to find unique solutions to clients' needs. Bermuda has a track record of firsts—the world's first captive insurers, the first excess liability carriers, the first property catastrophe insurers and "cat" bonds. With a population of approximately 65,000 people, the island attracts sophisticated clients who are interested in conducting business in a modern, well-regulated, solutions-oriented environment.

The Bermuda FinTech Strategy

It is against this economic backdrop that Bermuda's FinTech story began when in November 2017, the Government of Bermuda introduced a Blockchain Task Force comprising two groups who were charged with creating an ecosystem based on industry knowledge and an understanding of industry needs, while preparing Bermuda to be a leader in this new technological space. The vision was for Bermuda to introduce groundbreaking legislation, building on the island's sound reputation as a world-class regulator while understanding the requirements of business leaders in this new technology.

The Legal and Regulatory Working Group was tasked with developing a sound, appropriate legal framework to govern products and services related to FinTech. The group brought together international advisors and industry leaders with local regulators, technical officers, and experts to make sure the concerns surrounding digital assets were properly addressed through regulation.

Before Bermuda, there had been no jurisdiction equipped with the combined experience, innovation, agility, and determination to legislatively navigate the world of digital assets. This tiny island nation is proud to lead the charge, carving out a comprehensive regulatory future for the FinTech industry.

The Legislative Components

Initial Coin Offering Legislation

In April 2018, the Government of Bermuda made history by drafting and laying legislation in the House of Parliament that governs initial coin offerings (ICOs). Bermuda's Companies Act 1981 and the Limited Liability Company Act 2016 were amended to accommodate this new category of business. The legislation represents a strategic cornerstone of the Bermuda FinTech regulatory ecosystem.

In order to take advantage of Bermuda's regulatory framework, persons must first register a Bermuda-based company or a limited liability company (LLC) and be subject to the laws governing business entities in Bermuda. This also means that beneficial owners of entities seeking to launch their ICOs in Bermuda will be vetted by the Bermuda Monetary Authority and must meet Bermuda's stringent standards aimed at minimizing risks related to money laundering and terrorist financing.

Bermuda's business mandate is compliance, cooperation, and transparency, which means if a legitimate international tax authority requests information about the beneficial owners of a company, the information will be shared in accordance with the applicable treaty.

The legislation also sets forth the minimum requirements that will be applicable to all ICOs, regardless of the rights, functionality, or features of the digital asset offered for sale. In particular:

- There are requirements for the disclosure of information related to the rights and functionality of the digital assets, timelines for any project to be funded with ICO proceeds, and disclosure of any risks which may impact those who purchase the digital assets;
- There are specific requirements for the verification of the identities of everyone who purchases the digital assets, including cases where enhanced due diligence is required; and
- To ensure that purchaser identity information is available, as needed. There are also record-keeping requirements for such information.

An application for approval to issue an ICO from Bermuda must include a copy of the white paper, and will be subject to examination by a government-appointed Review Committee made up of legal, regulatory, and technology professionals. Applicants will be notified if additional information is needed or if additional laws will apply to the proposed issuance. If the entity meets the Bermuda Standard, the Government of Bermuda's Ministry of Finance will issue a consent to conduct the ICO.

The Digital Asset Business Act 2018

On Friday, May 11, 2018, two days after the passage of the ICO legislation, the Government of Bermuda tabled the Digital Asset Business Act in the House of Parliament. The Act has since been passed by the House of Assembly and Bermuda's Upper House, the Senate, and has also received the necessary assent for enactment.

This piece of legislation represents a world-first in providing comprehensive regulatory oversight for service providers of digital assets and associated products. With the passage of the Digital Asset Business Act, Bermuda has added a critical component to its FinTech strategy, while continuing to leverage what is deemed the Bermuda Standard.

The Digital Asset Business Act, which will be administered by the Bermuda Monetary Authority, is expected to serve as a global model of best practices for regulation of digital asset service providers. The Act is structured to be generally consistent with Bermuda's regulatory approach for other highly regulated business activities, and is modeled after Bermuda's Money Service Business Act 2016, the Insurance Act 1978, and the Investment Business Act 2003. It includes a tiered licensing structure, anti-money laundering (AML), and anti-terrorist Financing (ATF) protocols and prudential requirements, client asset protections, auditing requirements, and enforcement measures and powers.

Bermuda recognizes that the climate is challenging for transparency and the mitigation and prevention of financial crimes. As with the ICO legislation, anyone seeking a license under the Digital Asset Business Act will be required to first establish a traditional Bermuda company which will require vetting of the beneficial owners. The Act specifically requires that companies have a physical presence in Bermuda, including a senior representative who will be responsible for reporting specified information to the Bermuda Monetary Authority. Companies governed under the Act will also be subject to a number of requirements intended to mitigate risks related to financial crimes, consumer fraud, market manipulation, and unethical business practices.

It is imperative that Bermuda's reputation of being a well-regulated jurisdiction is preserved, and further enhanced with the country's entry into the FinTech space. As such, this comprehensive regime will be implemented in conjunction with regulations, codes of practice, statements of principles, and guidance similar to the legislative framework in place for other financial services regulated by the Bermuda Monetary Authority.

Banking Service for FinTech Companies

In the summer of 2018, Bermuda's Banks and Deposit Companies Act will be amended to create of a new class of bank that will provide services to Bermuda-based FinTech companies. The Bermuda Monetary Authority was consulted and supports the changes. The rationale for the introduction is that the FinTech industry's success globally depends on the ability of the businesses operating in this space to enjoy the necessary banking services. In other jurisdictions, banking has been the greatest challenge and therefore it had to be resolved with creative thinking and explored with new options.

National E-ID System

The Government of Bermuda is collaborating with leading technologists to create a national ID scheme for people and businesses. This will be a platform to help fulfill Know Your Customer (KYC) requirements in Bermuda. It will remove the need for multiple hard copies and handwritten signatures. Greater efficiencies will be realized together with business opportunities for the government, individuals, and businesses.

It is anticipated that E-ID will become a solid value-added addition to Bermuda's digital arsenal of business-friendly solutions.

Land Title Registration

In developing the legislation for the FinTech industry, Bermuda is developing blockchain solutions that improve vital government services for the country's citizens. In the first instance, all deeds will be put into an electronic format, replacing the current deeds-based system. With this advancement will be the opportunity to then place the deeds on blockchain, which will render the records immutable.

The Bermuda FinTech Innovation Hub

To foster and facilitate innovative thinking and creative solutions, the government is developing a purpose-built facility for technology companies that are domiciled in Bermuda to have access to a premium facility and support services. Companies will have access to a co-working space, private board room, lounge areas, high-speed internet, and concierge services.

Setting Up Business in Bermuda

Existing support agencies have been deployed to assist companies as they set up their business in Bermuda. The Bermuda Business Development Agency (BDA) is a critical first stop in setting up a business in Bermuda. As an independent entity whose mandate is to help raise Bermuda's profile through targeted business development activities which will help create jobs on the island, the BDA provides concierge services to help international companies set up, relocate, or expand their business in Bermuda.

The BDA connects prospective businesses to industry professionals and regulatory and government officials, providing options for corporate service providers and a legal support team for the company registration process. The BDA provides a single point of contact helping businesses to quickly and easily establish their presence in Bermuda.

Summary

Bermuda has partnered with key industry stakeholders putting in place memoranda of understanding which will prove mutually beneficial in the development of Bermuda's FinTech industry. The companies that incorporate a company in Bermuda will have revolutionary legislation to support their development and Bermuda will continue to be an incubator for advances in the industry.

Although this tiny island in the middle of the Atlantic is in the early stages of its FinTech strategy, Bermuda is leading the way by responding quickly to the market's needs and finding creative solutions that will allow FinTech companies to innovate in this nascent industry.

The Bermuda FinTech story is just starting. This account is a snapshot in time, as new developments and opportunities continue to evolve. Follow their progress at www.FinTech.bm.

Conclusion

One thing we know for certain is that technological advances will continue. These advances will create new marketplaces and evolve existing ones in real time. There will be more questions than answers in this space; therefore, there is a need to conduct more research on the impact of these emergent technologies and how they can benefit society. Topics that merit exploration include but are not limited to the following questions: Can the crypto marketplace evolve enough to become the global stock exchange of the future? Could crypto currency be used as an overlay to developing countries' currency backed by larger developed nations? Could crypto become an agnostic universal accepted currency for all types of business transactions? Could this currency provide access to wealth to underserved populations?

The future is here and those participants willing to accept the challenge and collaborate across industries will be the pioneers of this new frontier.

GPSR Compliance

The European Union's (EU) General Product Safety Regulation (GPSR) is a set of rules that requires consumer products to be safe and our obligations to ensure this.

If you have any concerns about our products, you can contact us on ProductSafety@springernature.com

In case Publisher is established outside the EU, the EU authorized representative is:

Springer Nature Customer Service Center GmbH
Europaplatz 3
69115 Heidelberg, Germany

Batch number: 10726233

Printed by Printforce, the Netherlands